Tolerance
the threshold
of peace

Tolerance – the threshold of peace

Note:

This unit is the first of a three-unit series.
The other two units are:

Unit 2:

Primary-school resource unit

Unit 3:

Secondary-school resource unit

Tolerance – the threshold of peace

Betty A. Reardon

Unit 1:
Teacher-training resource unit

The Teacher's Library

UNESCO Publishing

This resource is the result of the project in education
during the United Nations Year for Tolerance conceptualized and directed
by Ms Kaisa Savolainen, Director of the Section for Humanistic,
Cultural and International Education at UNESCO.

The author is responsible for the choice and the presentation
of the facts contained in this book and for the opinions expressed
therein, which are not necessarily those of UNESCO
and do not commit the Organization.
The designations employed and the presentation of materiel
throughout this publication do not imply the expression
of any opinion whatsoever on the part of UNESCO concerning
the legal status of any country, territory, city or area or of its authorities,
or concerning the delimitation of its frontiers or boundaries.

Published in 1997 by the United Nations Educational,
Scientific and Cultural Organization,
7, place de Fontenoy, 75352 Paris 07 SP.
Composed by Éditions du Mouflon, 94270 Le Kremlin-Bicêtre.
Printed by Imprimerie des Presses Universitaires de France, 41100 Vendôme.

ISBN 92-3-103376-X

Preface

Living with diversity is one of the greatest challenges facing the societies in which our children are growing up. In a world where cultures increasingly touch and intermingle, teaching the values and skills of 'learning to live together' has become a priority issue for education.

I therefore appeal to the world's Heads of State and Government, to Ministers and officials responsible for education at all levels, to the mayors of all cities, towns and villages, to all teachers, to religious communities, to journalists and to all parents:

- to educate our children and young people with a sense of openness and comprehension towards other people, their diverse cultures and histories and their fundamental shared humanity;
- to teach them the importance of refusing violence and adopting peaceful means for resolving disagreements and conflicts;
- to forge in the next generations feelings of altruism, openness and respect towards others, solidarity and sharing based on a sense of security in one's own identity and a capacity to recognize the many dimensions of being human in different cultural and social contexts.

In the follow-up to the United Nations Year for Tolerance celebrated on the initiative of UNESCO in 1995, it is crucial for all of us to continue to give new meaning to the word 'tolerance' and understand that our ability to value each and every person is the ethical basis for peace, security and intercultural dialogue.

A peaceful future depends on our everyday acts and gestures. Let us educate for tolerance in our schools and communities, in our homes and workplaces and, most of all, in our hearts and minds.

Federico Mayor,
Director-General of UNESCO

Jenny Frogner, 10, Norway

'A good teacher answers the needs of the pupils
and not only the chosen programme.'
Omar, 12, Morocco

Source: *What Makes a Good Teacher? Children Speak their Minds.*
Brochure of the International Children's Contest organized by UNESCO
through the Associated Schools Project, Paris, UNESCO, 1996.

Contents

 # FOR STUDY AND DISCUSSION

The purpose of this resource and how to use it

This volume is one of three produced by UNESCO as a contribution to the United Nations Year for Tolerance, 1995, and to the launching of the United Nations Decade for Human Rights Education (1995–2004). It is cast within UNESCO's Integrated Framework of Action on Education for Peace, Human Rights and Democracy which brings together within a comprehensive approach those three main elements as essential to a culture of peace. It recognizes, as does the Director-General's appeal, that education for tolerance within such an approach requires the active involvement of entire communities.

To facilitate this involvement, the material in this set of resources is presented to be of use and interest to various sectors of society. While the entire set emphasizes a rationale for and approaches to education for tolerance in primary and secondary schools, this first unit, the core conceptual resource, also addresses the social climate in which the schools educate in a manner that makes it especially useful in teacher education. But it acknowledges that many throughout the world, albeit not in schools, must also be educated for tolerance. Thus, it also suggests approaches for adult non-formal and community education. It is intended as study material for all who can help to educate for tolerance. This core resource can be used by classroom teachers, teacher educators, community leaders, parents, youth social workers and facilitators of adult education.

However, even this three-unit version of *Tolerance – The Threshold of Peace* does not pretend to be a complete curriculum or teaching guide. Rather, it is intended to be a catalyst and facilitator of the development of further materials designed for particular social and cultural contexts. UNESCO would appreciate reports on these efforts and copies of any curricular materials that result. From time to time, listings of such resources will be circulated to interested educators.

The lessons and projects included in the three units were selected from among those available at the time of the compilation of these three units. It is hoped that more educators will become involved in this effort to develop a 'pedagogy of tolerance'. We hope, too, that the descriptions of activities and the sample lessons in the two curriculum supplements will inspire educators to develop their own instructional materials and share them with UNESCO and others who may find them useful. UNESCO is grateful to all who sent comments on the preliminary version of *Tolerance – The Threshold of Peace* and materials to be reviewed for the preparation of this version and future-related publications.

While the narrative text reflects the suggestions and contributions of all the UNESCO sectors, its formulation is the responsibility of Dr Betty A. Reardon of Teachers College, Columbia University of New York (United States).

The conceptual material in all three texts is subject to copyright and may not be reproduced without permission. The curricular selections in the elementary and secondary supplements may be copied for classroom use only.

This volume and the two accompanying curriculum supplements have been prepared to serve as an introductory resource material, to provide some understanding of what is involved in and required of education for tolerance. Tolerance within the conceptual framework presented here is construed not as an end but as a beginning, an opening to a longer range and deeper process of peace-building. It provides a statement of the problems of intolerance, a rationale for teaching towards the goal of tolerance, and concepts and descriptions for identifying both the problems and the goals. These concepts are presented as behavioural indicators and social conditions in order to provide educators with the means to recognize the problems in their own contexts and to formulate goals appropriate to their own communities and classrooms. To aid in the pursuit of these goals, a learning process that places tolerance within the framework of education for peace, human rights and democracy is described and general learning goals are stated. Additional interpretations of these indicators and processes are offered in the curriculum supplements in formulations suited to the respective levels at which they are to be applied. Examples of various programmes of education for tolerance from all world regions are described in this core unit. Some of the means to carry out the programmes in classrooms are exemplified in teaching units in the two curriculum supplements, one for the primary and one for the secondary level.

Each chapter of this volume comprises material that can be used for study and discussion on issues of education for tolerance and peace. Organizations, community groups and formal classes of secondary level and above can use this material to explore together the issues raised and problems identified. The major audiences sought, however, are teacher educators and adult education facilitators.

It is hoped that special emphasis will be placed on discussion of possibilities for appropriate and constructive responses to overcome intolerance and initiate processes of peace-building in all classrooms and communities. Questions suggesting approaches to exploration of and responses to problems of intolerance are posed throughout. These questions and the text material in Chapters 1–4 are especially appropriate for use by adult and community groups, and in teacher education.

Chapter 5 describes a wide variety of examples of school-based projects and activities to educate for tolerance from all parts of the world. It also offers general guidelines and suggestions on where and how to integrate education for tolerance in elementary and secondary curricula as background for the two curriculum supplements.

Chapter 6 is addressed to non-formal adult educators, mainly describing efforts undertaken in popular education. Any community organization should find it of some use, and teachers in secondary schools and training colleges may also be able to adapt portions.

The appendices comprise references to resources that could be of use to anyone seeking to find materials and information relevant to education for tolerance.

We wish the users of this teaching/learning resource every success in their endeavours to educate for tolerance as the threshold to further and wider learnings for the achievement of peace, the fulfilment of human rights and the realization of democracy.

1. Why educate for tolerance?

Societies educate to serve socially constructive purposes. Often those purposes relate to particular goals or problems. As development education prepares citizens to participate in the processes of social, cultural and economic development, and environmental education provides instruction about the threats to the natural environment and encourages behaviour to overcome them, this set of three units is devised in that same perspective of education for socially constructive purposes. The larger society it is to serve is our emerging global community, in all its diversity. The social process it seeks to facilitate is peace-building through the observance of human rights and the practice of democracy. The problem it seeks to confront is intolerance, a severe and major threat to human rights, democracy and peace.

An epidemic of intolerance changes communities and challenges schools

World society, having emerged from the decades of the Cold War, enjoyed for a short time the hopes that the end of this struggle was the beginning of an era in which the destructive consequences of that conflict and the deep divisions imposed by global economic inequities might be addressed. These hopes were sorely tested, however, by the eruption of regional conflicts and the hostilities between peoples which fragmented nations and drastically changed the political map of the world as it had been for nearly half a century. All over the globe, intergroup tensions, religious hostilities and ethnic conflicts erupted. Many long-standing conflicts previously overlooked came to world attention.

Deep hatreds, some of which had previously healed over through reconciliations that permitted distinct ethnic groups to live together in peace and co-operation, surfaced in social behaviour and political movements, and were voiced in the media and at conferences; communities exploded into warfare. The process of settling the disputes, reconciling the hostilities and reconstructing the societies will be one of the most difficult human society has ever undertaken. It may be the greatest challenge ever faced by those who seek to educate for peace. Educators cannot shrink from facing the realities of history, nor can they avoid the responsibility of taking up the challenge posed by the reconciliation process to those who plan and carry out the social learning process.

These conflicts, along with problems of poverty that have accelerated migration rates, have swelled the numbers of refugees seeking asylum and migrants seeking work in countries and communities that once were primarily monocultural. Multiculturalism emerged, often unanticipated, as a social condition that affected many communities and had a major impact on their schools. Classrooms have become microcosms of the cultural diversity of global society and cross-cultural understanding has become a primary requirement of a healthy learning climate in schools around the world. For many schools, these new circumstances pose difficult challenges. Some have made of the challenges an opportunity to educate for a harmonious multiculturalism that is envisioned as the positive pluralism of a culture of peace, referred to in the secondary-level unit as a convivial community, or in the words of the distinguished Mexican educator Pablo Latapi, 'a community of solidarity'.

Cross-cultural understanding must be learned. Reconciliation must be learned. And each, in its turn, requires that tolerance be learned and practised. Such is the appeal of UNESCO's Director-General reproduced on the opening page of this resource.

Tolerance is integral to human rights and peace

As UNESCO's Director-General indicates, tolerance is integral and essential to the realization of human rights and the achievement of peace. In its most simple and fundamental form, tolerance is according others the right to have their persons and identities respected. The modern political and social values out of which the present international standards of human rights have evolved were first articulated in a call for tolerance as funda-mental to the maintenance of social order. The Western political philosophers articulated the necessity of tolerance to a society that could no longer tolerate the intolerance and strife of the religious wars of the sixteenth and seventeenth centuries. The recognition of tolerance as a fundamental component of peace among nations was a significant part of the historical climate that lead to the emergence of the first modern declarations of rights that culminated three centuries later in the Universal Declaration of Human Rights. In the Universal Declaration, the United Nations delineated the characteristics of the peaceful world order they envisioned in the form of rights, the fundamental claims all humans should be able to make upon society.

It has become apparent that much of the intergroup strife enflamed by intolerance derives from peoples' insistence on their rights to determine their own political, social and economic affairs. As the Universal Declaration points out, violence can be the consequence of the repression of democratic aspirations, just as it can be the result of intolerance. A major function of democracy is to facilitate political change and mediate political differences without violence. Thus, the element of democracy becomes essentially interlocked with peace, human rights and tolerance.

The achievement of these four values in the world society would constitute the basis of 'a culture of peace'. Any culture is fundamentally the result of learning. Education is the learning that is planned and guided by cultural values. A culture of peace thus requires an education planned and guided by the values of peace, human rights, democracy and, at its very core, tolerance. Given the present epidemic of intolerance, education for a culture of peace and programmes observing the United Nations Decade for Human Rights Education should focus on that essential value.

Who can help to educate for tolerance?

Every element of the community can contribute to educating for tolerance and every element can participate in observing the United Nations Decade for Human Rights Education.

Town councils could set up a week of events to celebrate the different groups in the community and what they have contributed to communal life. This observation might take place on 16 November, the day when UNESCO's Constitution was adopted, to observe the United Nations Decade for Human Rights Education. Various citizens' organizations and cultural groups could take responsibility for particular aspects of the observation.

Churches, temples, mosques, synagogues and religious organizations could organize programmes on religious tolerance, hold inter-religious dialogues, set up guidelines for teaching inter-religious respect in the community schools, and encourage study and discussion of United Nations standards on religious tolerance.

School authorities could introduce this resource to parents' and teachers' organizations, asking for suggestions about how the guidelines and directions could be adapted to the local situation and to understanding problems of intolerance and issues of human rights.

Parents and members of local organizations who have special experiences or knowledge of intolerance – what it is like and how to respond to it – or who work for human rights could volunteer to share these experiences in school assemblies and classrooms.

The role of the home and the family in the creation of tolerant and peaceful attitudes and respect for human rights is fundamental. Valuing peace in such a way as to motivate people to take the responsibility to act for peace is a crucial attribute of tolerance and peacefulness that can be most effectively developed in the home. Parents and caregivers need to be prepared to bring up the young in ways which will enable them to develop capacities for tolerance and peacemaking.

Community and social workers could develop action programmes to assess and confront problems of intolerance that affect their localities and clients.

Churches and schools could provide the venues for programmes to review and look for solutions to local issues and problems of intolerance in the community. Assistance to and solidarity with victims of intolerance on the part of parents and community are likely to be the most powerful instruction in education for tolerance that the young could receive.

Teacher educators, both pre-service and in-service, particularly those offering courses in the philosophical or social foundations of education, could use this resource as a supplementary text in their classes to introduce students and practising teachers to the concept of tolerance as an essential social value and an important learning goal for social education.

Many communities throughout the world have confronted their problems and produced solutions through popular education movements. Such movements view many of the problems that confront particular communities and the global society as problems of learning. They view learning in both its social and individual forms as essentially a participatory process. Individuals develop knowledge and skills which contribute to the capacity of communities to deal with their problems. Individuals taking up their communal responsibilities enter into programmes of co-operative learning through which they analyse and confront their common problems. For many communities, intolerance is such a problem and popular movements can therefore be major agents in educating for tolerance.

Teachers, teacher educators and non-formal educators could use this guide as a handbook for teaching methods, goals and guidelines. They are also urged to develop their own methods and materials to be shared with other educators and with UNESCO.

FOR STUDY AND DISCUSSION: ENVISIONING A WORLD OF TOLERANCE

The following questions and those in other chapters are formulated to help guide discussion among educators, especially those preparing teachers and those facilitating non-formal adult and community education programmes. They are appropriate for all concerned adults and some upper-secondary-school students:

▶ What kind of society might we have if we were to achieve a culture of peace? How might such a culture manifest itself in our family lives, communities, national politics and international relations?

▶ What relationship do you perceive between tolerance and peace? Could human rights be realized without a social commitment to tolerance? Is there, in your opinion, a significant relationship between human rights and democracy?

▶ What are your own personal and communal concerns about the issue of tolerance? How do these concerns relate to tolerance on a global scale? Can you make connections between your own concerns and the achievement of world peace?

2. Diagnosing intolerance and describing tolerance

Tolerance is not an end but a means

Tolerance is but the beginning, the first stage in a longer, deeper process of developing a culture of peace. It is the minimal essential quality of social relations that eschew violence and coercion. Without tolerance, peace is not possible. With tolerance, a panoply of positive human and social possibilities can be pursued, including the evolution of a culture of peace and the convivial communities that comprise it.

Intolerance and the cycle of violence

Intolerance derives from the belief that one's own group, belief system or way of life is superior to those of others. It can produce a range of consequences from a simple lack of civility or ignoring others, through elaborate social systems such as apartheid, or the intentional destruction of a people in the perpetration of genocide. All such actions originate in the denial of the fundamental worth of the human person. Thus *the overriding goal of education for tolerance is an appreciation of and respect for the human dignity and integrity of all persons*. This is the core value of all human-rights theory and international human-rights standards; it is the principal motivation behind efforts to achieve peace and the inspiration for democratic forms of government; it is the antithesis of intolerance.

Intolerance is a symptom that carries the potential of a life-threatening social illness – violence. Violence in human relations is usually avoidable and often intentional. It is a pathology that requires the mobilization of all possible efforts to protect the health and well-being of society. While 'preventive medicine' in the form of comprehensive lifelong education for peace, human rights and democracy is the most effective remedy, efforts also need to be made to respond effectively to the earliest symptoms. Policy-makers, educators, indeed all citizens, need to be able to recognize the symptoms or indicators of intolerance and to take appropriate action. Curative policies and actions must be designed and undertaken immediately the symptoms appear. Intolerance must be confronted if violence is to be avoided.

Symptoms of intolerance: general concepts for teaching about specific cases

Whatever the agent, be it a national government, a community organization, a school system or an individual teacher, who undertakes to educate for tolerance, that agent will need to assess and take into consideration in planning curative policies and actions the degree and type of intolerance that may be present in the environment in question. Indicators or 'symptoms' of intolerance can serve as tools for assessment and as a basis for teaching about intolerance. The symptoms defined below are listed somewhat in order of severity, but they do not represent a progression. One or more, or even all, may exist at the same time. Each, as it becomes apparent, serves as a warning that other symptoms may be present or are likely to follow, leading to a cycle of violence.

If these symptoms exist in a community, they probably exist in the schools. Teachers should be on the alert for them in their classrooms. To assist them in the diagnosis of the symptoms, the elementary curriculum unit presents the symptoms in terms of children's behaviour patterns. When children exhibit these symptoms in attitudes and behaviour in the classroom or playground, teachers should take note, but be prudent in their initial reactions. Children, especially younger ones, may be replicating attitudes from their homes and/or the community at large. They are seldom the originators of prejudices and dehumanizing attitudes and behaviour. When the behaviour is a blatant violation of rights, it may be dealt with directly, but even then it is important to refrain from preaching and moralizing, trying instead to explain and call for reflection on the consequences of the symptom.

In teaching how to recognize intolerance, it is useful to start with general descriptions and cases other than the actual ones that occur in the community where the teaching takes place. Then, through discussion and exploration, the teacher can lead into the elements of intolerance that directly relate to the students' own lives. The best of such teaching helps the students themselves to discover and 'name' these instances of intolerance. Students should always be helped to understand the general concepts defined in the following indicators as well as the specific examples, and be provided with information on other examples of the same concept. It is important that students recognize intolerance as a problem in many societies, a global problem, and that they realize that by addressing symptoms present in their schools and communities, they can contribute to reducing the severity of a worldwide problem, thereby gaining knowledge useful to themselves and to their societies over many years.

SOME SYMPTOMS OF INTOLERANCE AND THEIR BEHAVIOURAL INDICATORS

Language ➡ Denigrations and pejorative or exclusive language that devalues, demeans and dehumanizes cultural, racial, national or sexual groups. Denial of language rights.

Stereotyping ➡ Describing all members of a group as characterized by the same attributes, usually negative.

Teasing ➡ Calling attention to particular human behaviour patterns, attributes and characteristics so as to ridicule or insult.

Prejudice ➡ Judgement on the basis of negative generalizations and stereotypes rather than on the actual facts of a case or specific behaviour of an individual or group.

Scapegoating ➡ Blaming traumatic events or social problems on a particular group.

Discrimination ➡ Exclusion from social benefits and activities on primarily prejudicial grounds.

Ostracism ➡ Behaving as if others were not present or did not exist. Refusal to speak to or acknowledge others, or their culture (includes ethnocide).

Harassment ➡ Deliberate behaviour to intimidate and degrade others, often intended as a means of forcing them out of the community, organization or group.

Desecration and Defacement ➡ Forms of defacement of religious or cultural symbols or structures intended to devalue and ridicule the beliefs and identities of those to whom these structures and symbols are meaningful.

Bullying ➡ Use of superior physical capacity or greater numbers to humiliate others, deprive them of property or status, or force them into particular actions.

Expulsion ➡ Officially or forcefully expelling or denying right of entrance or presence in a place, social group, profession or any place where group activity occurs, including those upon which survival depends, such as places of employment or shelter, etc.

Exclusion ➡ Denying possibilities to meet fundamental needs and/or participate fully in the society, as in particular communal activities.

Segregation ➡ Enforced separation of people of different races, religions or genders, usually to the disadvantage of one group (includes apartheid).

Repression ➡ Forceful prevention of enjoyment of human rights.

Destruction ➡ Confinement, physical abuse, removal from area of livelihood, armed attacks and killings (includes genocide).

As any educator can readily recognize, some of these symptoms occur in all groups and arenas where intolerance can erupt. These forms of behaviour occur in schools from the earliest grades right through to the final years, even in universities. They also occur in businesses, other institutions and society at large. In introducing these concepts in a learning process, educators might begin with newspaper stories they have selected or that the learners or group members select. Try to describe various specific incidents so it is clear what actually constitutes the behaviour that points to intolerance. As indicated, the learning might start with more remote cases and ultimately come to 'storytelling' and reporting of the learners' own experiences and the instances of intolerance found in their own groups, classes and communities. Once the intolerance is recognized, responses should be addressed. It is best, however, to have some indicators of tolerance so that the responses can be directed not only at eliminating intolerance, but most especially at encouraging the development of tolerance. Such indicators are provided in the following section.

FOR STUDY AND DISCUSSION: MAPPING THE INTOLERABLE

Begin your study by reviewing the world situation of intolerance. If your class or study group meets regularly in the same place, put up a large world map and indicate on it (use colours or markers to show the same kinds of intolerance in various parts of the world) the following data:

- actual wars and armed conflicts between ethnic and/or language groups;
- such conflicts between religious groups who may be of the same ethnicity or 'race';
- racial conflicts and/or repression and segregation;
- conflicts between a minority or minorities and the majority, be it a political party, ethnic group or religion;
- incidents or conditions of violence against women or gender oppression;

▶ incidents of the systematic exploitation and/or abuse of children.

Make a bulletin board of photographs and magazine and newspaper accounts of cases and incidents of intolerance.

Select one intergroup conflict or outstanding example of intolerance for each of these areas: (1) Africa, (2) Asia, (3) the Pacific, (4) South and Central America and the Caribbean, and (5) North America and Europe; gather as much information on the cases you have selected as possible. Share the tasks of reading and reporting on the information among the class or group members.

Provide all members with copies of the Universal Declaration of Human Rights.

Discuss the following themes in relation to each case.

▶ Who are the groups involved?

▶ What evidence is there of intolerance? Here reflect on both the general symptoms or indicators of intolerance and the specific events and conditions showing that the symptom exists. Include dates, numbers of persons involved, specific harm done and human rights that have been violated.

▶ What are the issues? How would each of the groups involved describe what is at stake, and what their purposes and goals are? Would you or the parties argue that harm, other than or in addition to human-rights violations, has occurred? Describe the harm.

▶ What are the causes of the events and incidents? Are they recent or long-standing? What might each party identify as 'intolerable' in the other?

▶ What hopes do you see for resolution of the conflict? Development of tolerance in and between the conflicting parties? What needs to be achieved for a true resolution and reconciliation of the parties to the intolerance? Who can achieve it?

Make a list of conditions and problems in the world other than intergroup intolerance that you consider intolerable. Can these conditions be seen as violations of human rights? Do you think human-rights standards should be extended beyond the norms they now uphold to create a truly tolerant world society?

Nurturing signs of hope: the conditions of tolerance

Since conditions of tolerance do not readily seize our attention, we need to have some notion of how to recognize and encourage the practice of tolerance. Here, too, there are some indicators that can be used as both tools of assessment and the basis of designating goals for learning tolerance. If the indicated conditions of tolerance are not present in your class, school or community, educators and community leaders could initiate steps to integrate education towards their achievement into public policy guidelines and educational programmes.

SOME HOPEFUL SIGNS OF TOLERANCE AND THEIR SOCIAL INDICATORS

As defined here, these indicators refer to society at large, including all levels. In the curriculum supplement for elementary schools, they are described as characteristics of the tolerant classroom.

Language ➡ Absence of racial, ethnic and gender epithets. Media and texts use inclusive language and refrain from prejudicial adjectives and verbs in descriptions of events and people. Minority languages are employed in education and media.

Public order ➡ Characterized by equality among people, that is to say, equal access to social benefits, public activities, and educational and economic opportunities for all groups, men and women, racial, ethnic, religious, young and old, social classes, etc.

Social relations ➡ Based on mutual respect for the human dignity of all in society.

Political processes ➡ Essentially democratic with equal opportunity for participation of minorities, men and women.

Majority-minority relations and indigenous people ➡ The society or the particular group (school, business, etc.) intentionally provides space for exchanges between majority and minority groups, assures that the cultural integrity and languages of minorities are preserved and their use encouraged, and that human dignity and all rights of persons belonging to minorities and indigenous people are respected.

Communal events, historical observations, etc. ➡ Such public events involve everyone concerned in both planning and participation. Sensitivity to the historic consequences to all concerned is demonstrated in observing historical events, national holidays, etc.

Cultural events and manifestations ➡ All cultures of the society have opportunities to celebrate their traditions and are represented in all national and community cultural events.

Religious practices ➡ All are free to observe the practices of their religious faiths so long as the rights and integrity of others are respected. No one is required to participate involuntarily in religious observances.

Intergroup co-operation ➡ Common concerns of the entire community are addressed by all groups. Solutions to public problems and controversies are co-operatively sought by all groups, as are common social goals. Thus, inter-ethnic and inter-religious dialogues on common problems and group relations are part of the community discourse.

As these signs can be discerned in a society, it can be assumed that it is moving towards a culture of peace.

A culture of peace: aspirations and visions

The concept of a culture of peace inspires attempts to devise a comprehensive notion of a world at peace and to set goals and design plans for their implementation. There is still no one universal definition of a culture of peace; but many are seriously addressing the issue and seeking to describe such a culture. Participants in a UNESCO expert group meeting on 'Women's Contribution to a Culture of Peace' articulated their vision of a culture of peace. In this description, you will note various concepts and values that inform the curricula designed to educate for tolerance.

A culture of peace: aspirations and visions

The aspirations woven into [the participants'] visions of a culture of peace were expressed as a set of conditions that would prevail in such a culture.

A culture of peace would be a culture of freedom and universal respect, upholding all human rights and eliminating double standards. It can only be achieved within the context of equality between women and men.

A culture of peace would be a 'festival of diversities' which enriches the possibilities of achieving the human potential beyond accepting or tolerating difference; it would be based upon the diversities of different cultures and appreciation of 'the other', meaning complete refusal of dominance, exploitation and discrimination in all human relations and social structures.

A culture of peace would acknowledge the responsibilities of solidarity, in which the relief of the suffering of peoples is taken to be the responsibility of the entire world community. In a culture of peace, peoples are neither exploitable nor expendable. A culture of peace assures the dignity and the well-being of the vulnerable.

A culture of peace should be built upon the recognition of the realities of global interdependence, common human needs and common responsibility for the human future. There would be an end to the 'insider-outsider' mentality. In a culture of peace, the human person is enabled to develop the full range of human capacities unlimited by constraints of gender or other aspects of human identities.

In a culture of peace, persons would be educated to value human solidarity, mutuality and justice, and be provided with the skills to enable them to renounce violence as a means to achieve social or individual purposes. Values education would be pursued within the context of a global community that transcends the concept of separate competitive societies. The planetary society is but one unit, all is essentially 'inside' and education must develop consciousness of this unity to serve as a deterrent to violence.

In a culture of peace, power would be derived from shared capacities and responsibilities. Such a culture must be legally, politically, socially and morally inclusive, with power shared equally between women and men. Through a process of empowerment new strengths can be gathered for the achievement of the task of peace building.

In a culture of peace, conflicts need not produce violence; differences would be mediated in a spirit of mutuality; and disputes settled in ways which reconcile and strengthen communities. A culture of peace would recover and apply traditional, indigenous and women's modes of conflict resolution and notions of communitarian justice. In a culture of peace, there would be place for both ancient wisdom and new knowledge.

In a culture of peace, there would be space to express human creativity and share human feelings. There would be place for the sacred, acknowledging that 'the grove of trees is sacred, the river is sacred and we ourselves . . . are sacred.'

A culture of peace, valuing justice and pursuing sustainable development within a concept of sustainability that respects the integrity of cultures and the natural environment, would produce a social order based on equal human rights, the human dignity of all persons and reverence for living creatures and life systems.

Final Report of the UNESCO Expert Group Meeting on Women's Contribution to a Culture of Peace, Manila, 24–28 April 1995.

To educate for such a vision requires learning experiences to develop personal capacity for positive relationships; social responsibility for socially constructive behaviour; political efficacy for action to affect public policy; ethical maturity in making decisions about personal relations, social behaviour and political actions. It calls upon education to provide the major capacities for tolerance (see Table 2, Chapter 4, p. 53); living with diversity, dealing constructively with conflict, exercising responsibility.

FOR STUDY AND DISCUSSION: ASSESSING OUR OWN COMMUNITIES AND COUNTRIES

Most communities today are likely to manifest both symptoms of problems and signs of hope. Discuss in your class or citizens' group the following topics and questions to see where your community and nation stand with regard to tolerance.

▶ Give examples of signs of tolerance you have observed in your school, organization and/or community. What benefits result from these signs? What could be done to increase and strengthen these signs of tolerance? Can you and your class, organization or community undertake any of these actions?

▶ What specific symptoms of intolerance have you yourself observed or experienced? Describe the events and circumstances. What were the responses of the general public, those who suffered the acts of intolerance and those who committed them? Do you think these responses were 'healing' of the illness of intolerance or did they deepen its negative effects? What alternative responses can you think of? How could the indicators of tolerance be used to guide these responses? What results might be expected from these alternatives?

▶ Does your school, organization, community or nation have standards and guidelines to strengthen tolerance? If so, do any of them try to encourage forms of behaviour and practices listed among the signs of tolerance here? Are there other more effective guidelines or forms of behaviour? Are they applied and assessed? What other steps could be taken to reduce intolerance and build tolerance in your schools and communities?

▶ How would you describe a culture of peace?

Human rights: the limits of tolerance – restraint and responsibility

Tolerance is perceived as an abstraction. It is usually described as an attitude or a social condition. Neither definition, however, can be applied in the absence of the other. Tolerance as a social condition depends upon tolerance as an attitude widely held within the society. If tolerance is a condition sought or valued by a society, the attitude will be equally valued and regarded as a socially desirable attribute. Thus, as with all socially desirable attributes, the society will educate its people to value and exercise the attitude.

Even with the help of social indicators, tolerance is abstract, and hard to measure and observe. Intolerance is simple to see, especially when it results in the violation of human rights. We can easily assess the consequences of intolerance in embittered human relations, severely destructive social discrimination of all forms and its eruption into violent, frequently lethal conflict. But such is not the case with tolerance, for tolerance in its fundamental forms requires not only the observable conditions described in the previous section and explicit action to assure them; it also requires refraining from and restraining the destructive consequence of intolerance manifest in both personal behaviour and public policies. Tolerance is the very core of social responsibility in a pluralist society. It is the concepts and standards of human rights that specify the forms and goals of social responsibility and designate what conditions are intolerable and what forms of behaviour are to be restrained.

Tolerance can be viewed in both negative and positive terms. One aspect of tolerance is its being the antidote to intolerance. Negative, aggressive or exclusionary responses must be restrained within persons and societies. Indeed, the value of tolerance holds persons and societies responsible for such restraint. Human-rights standards and laws articulate some of these specific restraints in indicating what governments cannot do to citizens and what citizens must refrain from doing to other citizens. Such restraint is the minimal level of respect for others below which persons and societies fall into intolerance and the violation of human rights.

Positive tolerance calls for responsible action to create the conditions of tolerance that are integral to the realization of human rights and peace. In education, it calls for the cultivation of attitudes of openness, positive interest in differences and respect for diversity, sowing the seeds of the capacities for recognizing injustice and taking steps to overcome it, resolving differences constructively and moving from situations of conflict into reconciliation and social reconstruction.

Social manifestations of intolerance that violate human rights

The manner in which intolerance can be assessed as violations of human rights can be seen in some of the major forms of intolerance that have been addressed by human-rights movements, by international standards and by education for tolerance. The severe forms of intolerance defined here are significant components of violence. As such, they are of concern to educators, and motivate various educational efforts such as multicultural education. There is still need, however, for more curricula that deal directly with these issues.

SOME SEVERE FORMS OF INTOLERANCE

Sexism ➡ Policies and forms of behaviour that exclude women from full participation in society and from enjoyment of all human rights; rationalized by the assumption that men are intrinsically superior to women.

Racism ➡ Denial of human rights on the basis of race; rationalized by the assertion that some racial groups are superior to others.

Ethnocentrism ➡ Exclusion on the basis of culture or language; rationalized by the notion of different levels of value and 'advancement' among cultures.

Anti-semitism ➡ Attitudes and behaviour of prejudice, discrimination and persecutions perpetrated against Jews.

Aggressive nationalism ➡ Belief that one nation is superior and has rights over others.

Fascism ➡ Belief that the state should not tolerate dissent or diversity and has the authority to control the lives of citizens.

Xenophobia ➡ Fear and dislike of foreigners and those of other cultures; belief that 'outsiders' will harm the society.

Imperialism ➡ Subjugation of one people or peoples by another, for control of the subjugated people's wealth and resources.

Exploitation ➡ Use of people's time and labour without fair recompense; imprudent and wasteful use of resources and the natural environment.

Religious fanaticism ➡ Enforcement of a particular faith or its values and practices (sometimes on entire communities) and the favouring of members of that faith over others; rationalized by the notion that the faith in question is the only authentic interpretation of religious or spiritual truth, and its tenets must be followed without exception.

Political repression ➡ Prevention of free and open discussion of political ideas and policies; posing obstacles to political participation, and to free and fair elections; limitations on freedom of information; severe punishment of political dissidents.

FOR STUDY AND DISCUSSION: USING HUMAN RIGHTS TO DIAGNOSE INTOLERANCE

The entire group or class should read and study the Universal Declaration of Human Rights, then discuss together the following topics and questions:

▶ What conflicts between ethnic and religious groups could be avoided or resolved through observing human rights? Which rights in particular?

▶ Which of the rights in the Declaration call for restraint of certain forms of behaviour and conditions, and which for active responsibility?

▶ Review the social conditions of intolerance that violate human rights and suggest responses that call for restraint and responsibility. What must be stopped? What must be done?

▶ Add to your map of the intolerable in the world indicators of where there is evidence of the social manifestations and beliefs that support intolerance. Describe the evidence and its human consequences.

▶ What movements exist to overcome these manifestations of intolerance? Are such movements uniformly tolerated in all cases where the intolerance prevails? What are appropriate ways to respond to these manifestations?

▶ Research the declarations, covenants and conventions that make up the international standards for the protection of human rights. Which of them were intended or could be used to overcome the severe forms of intolerance described and listed here?

3. Problems and possibilities of educating for tolerance

Tolerance is a complex and controversial subject. Educators committed to its realization will have to confront many problems, including not only the conditions of intolerance previously described, but also the varying and contrasting concepts and perceptions of tolerance that can obscure its meaning and the social conditions that make tolerance appear to be an almost impossible goal. For example, since the eighteenth century, tolerance has been identified as a positive social attribute by the Christian West. However, in other cultures it is viewed differently. According to Venerable Prayudh Payutto, the Buddhist monk who was awarded the 1994 UNESCO Prize for Peace Education, tolerance is a negative ethic because it has certain elements of restraint, enforcement and compromise. Tolerance is, therefore, not enough to maintain peace. Many aspects of the human personality must be addressed in the formation of peace-makers.

Buddhism identifies three self-centred motives which lead people into intolerance, conflict and peacelessness: selfish desire; lust for dominance and insistence on one's own views, faith and ideology; and egocentrism. The unchecked drive for power and wealth leads us into conflict and violence, but this drive can be overcome.

To achieve peace, human beings need to strive to overcome some of these tendencies which are similar to those we have identified as symptoms of intolerance: aggressive nationalism, ethnocentrism, exploitation/ colonialism and racism. Education can help us to do so. Many citizens and educators, as demonstrated in Chapters 5 and 6, hold positive visions of the possibilities for a tolerant society and are taking action and educational initiatives to achieve these possibilities.

Vagaries and varieties of definitions

Tolerance is hard to describe, perhaps because it is defined somewhat differently from language to language, even in the official languages of the United Nations, as can be seen from the list reproduced here:

Tolerencia: (Spanish) The capacity to accept ideas or opinions different from one's own (*Diccionario planeta de la lengua española usual*).

Tolérance: (French) An attitude which grants that others may think or act in a manner different from that of one's self (*Le Petit Robert* dictionary).

Tolerance: (English) Willingness to tolerate, forbearance.

Tolerate: Endure, permit (practice, action, behaviour), allow (person, religious sect, opinion) to exist without interference or molestation . . . allowing of difference in religious opinions without discrimination (*Concise Oxford Dictionary of Current English*).

Kuan rong: (Chinese) Allow, admit, to be generous towards others.

Tasamul': (Arabic) Pardon, indulgence, lenience, clemency, mercy, mercifulness, forbearance [. . .] accepting others and forgiving.

Tolerantnost, terpimost: (Russian) Ability to tolerate (to endure, bear, stand; put up with) something or somebody, that is, to admit/accept the being, existence of something/somebody, to reconcile oneself to something/ somebody, to be condescending, lenient to something/somebody.

Each of these definitions reveals differences in emphasis, culture and historical experience. They are evidence of the very diversity that pluralism values. Each also encompasses the fundamental essence of tolerance: that is, to respect the rights of others – 'the different' – to be who they are, to refrain from harm because harming 'the other' means harm to all and to the self. In tolerance, there is the intuition of the unity and interdependence of humanity, a unity and interdependence that the ecological age has taught us to see as encompassing all humankind and the whole planet, and this has facilitated a holistic view of the world and education that informs the approaches to teaching for tolerance advocated here.

So, despite these nuances of meaning, there is enough communality among the languages quoted for the concept of tolerance to provide a common base for practice. Specifically, there is a common recognition that tolerance is a necessity both of civil society and for the very survival of humanity.

While the *concept* of tolerance is controversial, the *practice* of tolerance is not. In the Preamble to the Charter of the United Nations, the stated goal is indeed 'to practise tolerance' for the maintenance of peace, justice, respect for human rights and the promotion of social progress. Tolerance can exist in its most active form only in a setting in which human dignity and civil liberties are respected.

Proclamation of the United Nations Year for Tolerance and Declaration on Tolerance, Paris, UNESCO, 1993 (doc. 27C/25).

Problems and pitfalls: obstacles to overcome in teaching for tolerance

Given the climate of the world in which there is so much intolerance, there are bound to be significant problems to face when communities, schools and teachers undertake education for tolerance. These problems are mainly, but not exclusively, social and pedagogical.

All education related to peace, human rights and democracy is essentially values education. Values continue to be a source of potential problems for educators in that even the most widely held values are subject to varying interpretations, and often parents and others in the community perceive such education as threatening to the systems of values they seek to impart to their children. Educators need a great deal of preparation in understanding and responding fairly and constructively to these responses as well as in appropriate methods and approaches to conceptualizing and instructing in the fundamental human values validated by United Nations standards on human rights. Values education requires the involvement of entire education systems and the communities they serve.

The potential pitfall in values education was recognized in the guidelines issued by UNESCO's Principal Regional Office for Asia and the Pacific, emphasizing the need for constant monitoring and regular evaluation of values education.

Guidelines for managing values education

Values education requires more attention because its implementation involves various parts of the school organization and a number of teachers of various disciplines. This implies that there must be effective co-ordination and communication to make the values education programme more meaningful for the school and for the students. Considering this argument it is necessary for the school administrator and the teachers to put more attention to the following guidelines.

> *Guideline 1:* Values education at school must be clearly stated in the school curriculum policy and there must be a co-ordinator for all values education programmes at the school.
>
> *Guideline 2:* A certain amount of funds must be allocated to support the implementation of the values education programmes at the school.
>
> *Guideline 3:* Regular and continuous discussions and consultations among values educators must be carried out to monitor the progress, identify problems and seek out proper solutions to the problems.
>
> *Guideline 4:* Values educators must continuously analyse the appro-priateness of the integration of certain core values into certain entry points of various subject matters, identify problems, and select proper solutions to the problems for the improvement of the implementation of the curriculum integration.
>
> *Guideline 5:* The selection and the adoption of certain teaching strategies must be continuously monitored and evaluated with respect to the effectiveness of the strategies.
>
> *Guideline 6:* Values educators must monitor and solicit responses of students concerning questions on certain values. This is important for further values clarification in the teaching/learning processes.
>
> *Guideline 7:* Education media such as various audiovisual aids and other learning resources must be prepared every time values education sessions are to take place. This is essential to support the effectiveness of the strategies employed.
>
> *Guideline 8:* Values educators must continuously work together in designing and developing evaluation instruments needed to evaluate the learning outcomes of values education processes.
>
> *Guideline 9:* A comprehensive report on the implementation of values education programmes must be prepared regularly every semester and presented to the school administrator for review and evaluation. Such review and evaluation are essential for policy improvement.
>
> Mohammed Fakry Gaffar, *Guidelines for Implementing the Prototyped Curriculum of Core Values for Enhancing International Understanding, Co-operation and Peace*, Bangkok, UNESCO Principal Regional Office for Asia and the Pacific, 1995.

Prejudice:
a common attitude

There are few human beings who do not harbour some prejudices. The goals of self-awareness and self-esteem as well as that of creating tolerant social relationships call on all individuals to become more conscious of these prejudices, to discover their origins and to understand how they affect our thinking and our behaviour. When teaching about prejudice as a form of intolerance and a cause of negative discrimination, teachers need to be sensitive to several crucial factors that may affect their students and the atmosphere of their classes.

They must be aware of their own prejudices, of course, and of the possibility that some of the students may in fact be the victims of prejudice as well as the perpetrators of discrimination based on prejudice. This problem can be faced as an issue of how we think and how we may become more effective thinkers and so become more responsible citizens. Thus, prejudice must in the first place be identified as a fallacious or limited mode of thinking – prejudgement. Responsible citizens make judgements on the basis of sound information.

However, the teacher certainly needs to acknowledge that prejudice is for the most part an emotional response often based on stimuli and factors of which we are not truly aware. So teachers might be well served by thinking of education about and against prejudice more as a consciousness raising than as an instructional process. It is a process in which they themselves can engage as learners with their students as indicated in the advice offered by the Minority Rights Group (see Unit 3, p. 38).

Violence and bullying in schools

Violence in schools is another major problem confronting education for tolerance. It appears to be a major problem in many parts of the world. Much school violence is the consequence of bullying, a form of behaviour identified in this resource as a symptom of intolerance. Bullying is dealt with in some detail with suggestions from Japan on how teachers can deal with the problem in the Curriculum Supplement for Secondary Schools, Selection 4. The following suggestions from New Zealand are for school administrators and school systems.

Violence in schools includes physical, verbal and emotional assaults. It is often called bullying and used to be seen as part of growing up but it should not be dismissed in this way. Bullying has negative consequences for both the victim and the bully. Research suggests that it exists in [many] schools. . . .

Schools can intervene effectively to stop bullying. Parents or caregivers who are concerned about a child being bullied should raise the matter with the school. The following are some suggestions about how a school community can respond to bullying.

How can a school intervene effectively to reduce violence?

- acknowledge the problem;
- establish an anti-violence atmosphere;

Various programmes identify the steps that should be taken in developing an anti-violence atmosphere. These might include;

- conducting a survey to establish the extent of the problem;
- sharing the results with staff and pupils:
- establishing school rules in consultation with students and parents;
- designing a school contract between staff and pupils;
- involving relevant outside organizations.

Strategies for dealing with violence

- Make a commitment to always intervene when violence is suspected or identified.
- Include elements of non-violence teaching in all relevant parts of the curriculum.
- Initiate anti-violence programmes.
- Ensure that adults do not model violence.
- Develop and follow procedures which encourage the reporting of violence and its investigation.
- Respond thoroughly to reports of bullying.

Students and parents should expect:

- to be heard and responded to sensitively and without being dismissed out of hand;
- to be told that all forms of violence are against school policy and reminded what the policy is;
- to be told that the report will be investigated and that there will be a response, that they will receive feedback on the situation reported, and that the incident will be responded to in a way appropriate to its nature;
- that they will be provided protection from negative consequences of their reporting;
- that the school will intervene and support victims and respond to perpetrators.

- Identify a range of strategies and services to help both the perpetrators of violence and the victims.
- Monitor the policy and programmes.

Beth Wood and Andrea Jamison, *Students Rights at School*, Wellington, New Zealand Office of the Commissioner for Children.

Constructive conflict resolution to prevent violence

One way many schools have undertaken to deal with violence is the teaching of non-violence and conflict resolution. A number of curriculum selections in both Units 2 and 3 deal with these methods. Indeed, developing a capacity for constructive handling of conflict is designated as a significant learning goal of education for tolerance. The American Friends Service Committee in Kansas City, an agency which trains teachers in how to teach these skills, makes the following recommendations:

Create a co-operative, tolerant, supportive classroom environment which:

- helps children feel important, valued and unique;
- allows children to function with the maximum degree of freedom possible;
- helps children feel safe, comfortable and trusting;
- supports the development of friendship, empathy and respect for the needs and feelings of other children;
- structures opportunities in which children work and play co-operatively and successfully together;
- provides recognition for accomplishments and differences;
- gives opportunity for children to understand themselves, communicate their ideas and feelings, and develop an understanding of others;
- produces opportunities for the development of social skills through dramatic and co-operative play.

Model the positive behaviour you would like the children to learn:

- positive self-esteem, empathy and tolerance;
- constructive conflict attitudes and co-operation;
- good listening skills;
- assertive communication skills;
- problem-solving.

Teach, reinforce and infuse:

- social skills;
- positive self-esteem;
- constructive conflict resolution skills.

Establish special activities such as peer mediation, class meetings and peer helpers and infuse skills and attitudes into all areas of your curriculum.

Some suggestions for establishing a peer mediation programme

Planning and staff support: the thoughtful development of a program designed to meet both student and staff needs is essential.

Teaching the basic skills of conflict resolution: establishing a two- to four-week period of time when all classroom teachers take twenty to thirty minutes a day to teach basic conflict resolution attitudes and skills: (1) self-esteem; (2) attitudes and beliefs about conflict; (3) strategies and dynamics of conflict; (4) communication skills; (5) expressing emotions and dealing with anger; (6) problem-solving skills.

Modelling: instruction needs to be re-enforced by teacher modelling.

Infusion and integration: it is not necessary to add conflict resolution as an additional ongoing subject area. Rather set conflict resolution objectives for regular lessons along with the content objectives.

Effective mediation training, monitoring, and ongoing training: making the sessions very positive and open. Mediation training should follow classroom conflict resolution instruction. It should include plenty of small group role-playing.

Following these suggestions and listening to each other's concerns and ideas will help ensure that your conflict resolution and mediation programs help students solve their conflicts and gain skills which they can use throughout their lives!

Ira Harritt, Kansas City American Friends Service Committee Program Co-ordinator, United States.

Guidelines for teaching about religion

Religion is a significant factor in the evolution of cultures, providing both meaning, and behavioural and social codes. Sadly, it has also been the basis of divisions, intolerance and conflict, so that teaching for religious tolerance is an urgent necessity. However, teaching about religion remains problematic in some countries.

The following guidelines are based on some of the ones developed for the schools of a primarily Christian community in Northern Ireland, where religious intolerance has caused severe suffering and violence. They could, however, be adapted to other communities.

Children should be introduced first to those aspects of various religions which they are likely to enjoy and admire. For example, in introducing a study of Islam, looking at Muslim art and architecture or examples of Arabic script is more likely to be appealing than starting with practices or beliefs. If they find Muslim geometric patterns and Arabic script fascinating, they are much more likely to take a positive interest in other aspects of the religion. . . .

The pupils should be learning about living religions. The emphasis should, therefore, be on what it is like to be Buddhist, Muslim, Jew or Hindu, Sikh, Zoroastrian, Baha'i or Christian today. We have to resist the temptation to deal first with the origins of a religion, which would be far too complex a subject for children of primary-school age to understand without distortion.

It is important to acknowledge the wider culture within which beliefs, values, customs, and rituals have their place. With young people, more emphasis should be placed on this wider social context. . . . On the whole, it is preferable to think of the people rather than the '. . . ism'.

Where there are pupils of various faiths in the school, they could participate as 'resource persons' sharing their beliefs and practices with their classmates. Their participation will give a sense of reality to the study. Both they and the learning process will benefit.

Central to the purpose of studying religions with appreciation and respect is the ideal of helping pupils to stand where the believer stands, to see what his religion must look – and feel like – to him or her, how it affects her life and society. This, of course, can never be fully achieved 'at a distance'. But with due attention to questions of accuracy, objectivity and respect, we may hope to come nearer to the ideal in teaching world religions.

Maureen Ryan, *Handbook on Introducing World Religions in the Primary Schools.* Available through Education for Mutual Understanding (Belfast, n.d.).

A particular approach to teaching about world religions is given in Unit 2, pp. 70–1, of this guide.

Philosophy and fanaticism: ethical education for tolerance

Much of the religious intolerance in the world today stems from a way of thinking that insists there is one truth and one correct way of interpreting it. That way may be based on religious interpretation as well as on political ideology or a fixed interpretation of aspects of social organization, such as gender roles, which reinforce male dominance, fanatically adhered to as the only way to be truly human. Whatever the basis, these forms of fanaticism seek to impose a limited vision of the world on their societies. They devalue diversity and limit the full development of the human person.

In some instances, such forms of thinking are passed on to the young through an education that cultivates intolerance, and limits the cognitive and creative capacities of the learners. Above all, education for tolerance requires education for well-reasoned and truly reflective thinking, forms of thinking that encourage consideration of alternatives, and of the moral and practical consequences of actions. Such forms of thinking are currently being provided through programmes not only in conflict resolution (which emphasize the consideration of alternatives and consequences), but also in philosophy (which emphasize moral reflection).

It has been argued that moral education is essentially education in philosophy and that education in philosophy is the most effective preparation for the practice of democracy, and the realization of human rights.

Philosophy as the free pursuit of inquiry cannot consider any truth to be final and encourages respect for the convictions of the individual but should in no circumstances, at the risk of denying its own nature, accept doctrines which deny the liberty of others, affront human dignity and sow the seeds of barbarity.
Philosophy (newsletter of the UNESCO Division of Philosophy), No. 1, 1995, p. 2.

As can be seen from the foregoing quotation, UNESCO supports the inclusion of philosophy as a form of education for citizenship in a diverse world society, as something of practical necessity for education to address the kind of issues raised by the problems of intolerance.

Philosophy is not obscure. Indeed its primary goal is to shed light on ideas. Its tasks are to clarify, make distinctions and arrive at conclusions by reason. Such tasks are demanding and are, increasingly, of universal value: providing the largest possible number of people with a grounding in philosophical inquiry is a way of serving freedom.

Without knowing the answers, philosophers can offer tools for a more incisive analysis of contemporary situations. Training in philosophy, which enhances the capacity for independent judgement, must be developed in the field of education.
Ibid., p. 1.

Philosophy as a form of moral education has been conducted at all levels of elementary and secondary education, carrying out the concepts described below by Ann Margaret Sharp, a Canadian educator, who has worked in this field for some years.

If children could learn to do philosophy well in their formative years, they could acquire the skills that they need not only to shape their lives in a harmonious fashion, but to think, judge and act well with regard to the good of all. If Aristotle was correct that ultimately all moral judgements are related to the adequacy of our perceptions, then it follows that the education of perception is essential. Doing philosophy within the context of the community of inquiry encourages students to cultivate their perception, that is, to become better at discerning acutely and responsively the salient features of their particular situation before making a moral judgement. It is this ability that is at the core of practical wisdom.

What is children's philosophy?

Philosophy for Children is an attempt to take the discipline of philosophy and reconstruct it for children in such a way that they can appropriate the concepts and methods and come to think for themselves about matters of importance, while at the same time, *care* about doing so. With its curriculum that ranges from day care centre age to 18 years of age, it aims to acquaint children with the tools that are required to think well about their own thinking while at the same time discussing philosophical issues that arise in their own experience. The focus is on the *doing* of philosophy rather than learning about philosophical systems or specific philosophers of the past. One will find most of the ideas of the major philosophers of the West, and some of the East (hardly enough) presented in a dialogical mode that encourages children to think for themselves about the meaning of these ideas.

What are these virtues or strengths of philosophy – both practice and content – that carry over from the traditional academic, higher education version of philosophy to children's philosophy?

1. Ethical *inquiry*. Engaging children in investigation of problems dealing with the role of moral values and norms in human conduct.
2. Aesthetic *inquiry*. Engaging children in exploring problematic issues that involve the relationships between artistic creation, aesthetic appreciation and aesthetic criticism.
3. Metaphysical *inquiry*. Encouraging children to reach for greater and greater generality in their understanding of the world and its ways of working.
4. Logical *inquiry*. Engaging children in reflection on the rules of inquiry, and into whatever principles are appealed to when thinking about thinking.
5. Epistemological *inquiry*. Having children seek to answer such questions as 'What counts for true?' and 'What is the relationship between truth

and meaning?' (Lipman, *Is Philosophy Needed in the Primary School?*, 1993).

Philosophy also provides children with a rigorous methodology of linguistic and logical analysis which will stand them in good stead as they assume more responsibility in society.

Extract from Ann Margaret Sharp, *Philosophy for Children and the Development of Ethical Values* (paper presented at the Foro Internacional Educación y Valores, 25–27 May 1994, Museo Nacional de Antropología, Mexico City).

Encouraging reflection on essentially moral issues can in fact begin with very young children, as can be seen in a French publication on education for peace in infants' schools.

Working against conformism and developing children's autonomy are also ways in which to work towards peace. Such autonomy can be a goal from birth and will produce well-suited but independent beings capable of managing their own future. It will develop that essential sense of relativity which enables a level-headed view to be taken of past experience so as to avoid involvement in conflicts whose rationale eventually becomes obscured.

We have split the issues into three themes:
- conflicts, friendship, understanding war and peace;
- racism;
- hunger and destitution.

Each project, modest though it may be, is a source of vitality opening up new vistas for the future.

Maryse Michaud, *Enfance et partage*, Paris, Centre Départemental de Documentation Pédagogique du Val-de-Marne, 1985.

Similar efforts are being made in other parts of the world. For example, the national curriculum of Thailand includes two courses that reflect the same concerns and approaches outlined here. Both are offered at the lower secondary level in the social studies course. The first is 'Ethics of Selected Individuals' based upon the lives and works of morally upright individuals who are creative in bringing progress to their communities, the society and the nation. Students are guided in analysing moral ethics, behaviour guidelines and lines of thoughts of such people affecting development of themselves, the community and the country.

The objective is to enable learners to see good models of behaviour, appreciate the merits of employing moral ethics to guide one's way of life, and be able to choose proper practices to develop themselves, the communities and the country.

Social Studies Curriculum for Lower Secondary Education Level (1990 Revision), Ministry of Education of Thailand.

The second, 'Lives and Work of Selected Outstanding Individuals', involves studying about lives, works and lines of thoughts of important individuals who have affected social changes or the human condition both at the national and world levels.

The objective is to enable learners to develop knowledge and understanding about ways of life, working procedures, and work efforts of such persons; appreciate the ideas and works beneficial to the society and the human race; and see prospects for self-improvement, and improvement of the society.

Ibid.

Sensitive and complex social climates require education for moral decision-making and social responsibility

Most current programmes of education for tolerance have been inspired by problems of rapidly changing societies, making more urgent the need for philosophic and/or moral education. Communities are faced with problems of relations between groups who have had little or no previous contact. These relations are initiated in a context of cultural ignorance (each knowing little or nothing of the other), economic stress with community resources stretched beyond their limits and increasing problems of unemployment, lack of housing and other amenities. In too many cases, these situations have been exacerbated by racial, religious and ethnic prejudices, by past hostilities between some groups and by a reawakening of an exclusionary sentiment of chauvinism. Residual and renewed religious intolerance has intensified, and religious discrimination, segregation and conflict undermine national unity and pose severe problems of human relations especially challenging to schools.

Media violence is a very significant element of the social climate and may well contribute to violence in the schools. Among young children who have little or no knowledge of how to deal constructively with conflicts and differences, the negative impact of the images of violence portrayed in the 'entertainment' media has been noted with deep concern. Children are often frightened by these images and even more often use them as models of behaviour in conflictual situations. Of special concern is the violence evident in the cartoons designed for and directed at young children. Educators seeking to develop tolerance and respect for others have to begin with the youngest children, offering lessons to help them become more morally aware and critical of these images and the behaviours they portray. (One such French effort to do so is described in Maryse Michaud (ed.), *L'éducation à la paix*, Paris, Centre National de Documentation Pédagogique, 1994.)

Violence has also been a consequence of the rise of ideologies of hatred often inspired by some of the above-mentioned forms of fanaticism that seduce the young into political movements against immigrants and the culturally different. Those who seek to educate for tolerance will need sensitivity to the cultural, economic and ideological complexities of the community, and a very close acquaintance with the fears, perceptions and attitudes of the young. Many youths see a future not only of joblessness but of purposelessness, a life with little reward and no meaning. The situation faced by young people is among the elements of the intolerable that threaten all the value goals advocated here. Education for tolerance needs to address the issue of assuring the young that their teachers, if not their societies as a whole, are committed to achieving a tolerable future for coming generations.

The primary arena for persuading the young of possibilities for a more positive future is that of moral education, an education in which they are helped to see that many of the problems of intolerance and deprivation they face can be resolved through the application of ethical standards to social relations and public policy. The situations we confront in the world today are the result of choices, many of them made on the basis of power and pragmatism abstracted from morality. The degree of human suffering tolerated in the world is evidence of our failure to insist on the fulfilment of the moral standards nations have agreed to in the covenants and treaties intended to bring a tolerable level of civility to world society. Historical and current experience tells us that change towards humane conditions can occur when these standards are invoked and pursued in appropriate ways.

No matter what the subject, however, the ethical dimension should always be included; effects on the fundamental value concepts of peace, human rights and democracy, and the core value of human dignity should be assessed in the making of every choice. Ethical choice-making, as noted, can best be learned through the practice of choice-making. All learners, most especially children and adolescents, should receive an education that provides them with opportunities for making moral choices about personal and social issues.

We know that the internalization of moral standards is strengthened by action and application of the standards to actual situations. Education for tolerance should include occasions on which the young can take action towards the realization of the values they claim to uphold. These occasions should be authentic, in the context of a problem that is of direct concern to them (that concern can often be a global issue when the students see its relevance to their own lives and values) and they should have the opportunity to reflect on the consequences of these actions.

Confronting the consequences of their own negative values, and the intolerance they condone or practise, can also be effective. One case of such a lesson was organizing a visit to Auschwitz for some young 'skinheads'. Learning for moral responsibility is most productive in a cycle of information-gathering, moral and practical reflection, decision-making, action and evaluative reflection. The cycle should be ongoing and continuous in whatever ways are possible and appropriate at all levels and in all spheres of education. Indeed, this cycle of study, moral reflection, social action, and further reflection and study is the core of the lifelong learning process necessary to achieve and maintain tolerance and democracy.

FOR STUDY AND DISCUSSION: PREPARING FOR MORAL REFLECTION

While all groups and classes can consider the following questions, the first three most concern schools, and the fourth concerns the community and teacher education.

▶ Does your school or community face problems of chauvinism and alienation among the youth? What efforts are being made to help the young gain capacities for facing their problems?

▶ What situations and problems would be most appropriate to learning experiences for moral choice making in your group or class? What standards and criteria would you establish for the morality and efficacy of your choices and actions?

▶ Do you believe that the study of philosophy can improve students' capacities for independent critical thinking and moral decision-making? Would such education be appropriate to the schools of your community?

▶ Are the teachers or your schools given pre- and in-service education in discussion techniques and moral education? How can the community and the other school personnel help teachers in developing these capacities?

4. Tolerance in the school: a laboratory for the practice of tolerance

The framework, goals and teaching approaches presented in this resource demonstrate that education for tolerance is: (a) based on sound pedagogical principles, (b) a vehicle for the achievement of the general purposes of education; and (c) a social necessity. Communities can thus support and mobilize for introducing tolerance education into schools because it is responsible, appropriate and necessary education.

The school: socializing agent and community centre

School or 'schooling' in the sense of intentional instruction that socializes children and youth, whether it takes place within or outside a formally constituted school, is the most direct means for teaching social values. Thus, it is this institution in whatever form it takes that must assume much of the responsibility for education towards social goals.

As community leaders, parents, school authorities, teacher educators and teachers direct their attention to the planning and implementation of a programme of education for tolerance, the school becomes the focus of the education of entire communities. So it is that this resource focuses on the school but also addresses the wider community. For the school has been, and in some parts of the world still is, a community centre. Not only do communal activities take place in schools, but it can be in the envisioning, planning and preparing for the future of the young that communities can come together in the formulation and pursuit of their communal goals.

Schools therefore can be arenas of community-building as well as of instruction for tolerance. They must be places in which tolerance is practised as well as taught.

Principles for the practice of tolerance in schools

If schools are to be such places, they will need principles and guidelines for tolerance.

The following is a list of the 'ingredients' of anti-racist education as it is being developed by the Anne Frank Foundation (the Netherlands). It provides an excellent list of principles for education for tolerance:

1. School responsibility (to educate for tolerance).
2. Positive approach to ethnicity.
3. Learning to think inclusively.
4. Integrating intercultural education.
5. Focusing on similarities.
6. Combating racism on a broad front.
7. Creating a positive school atmosphere.

A tolerant classroom climate

Just as the society at large and the school as the institutional agent of education must be organized for and exemplify the values and practices of tolerance, each classroom should also be an environment for nurturing tolerant attitudes and for developing the capacities to practise them. The following process model taken from New Zealand exemplifies forms of behaviour practised in the tolerant (positive) and intolerant (negative) classrooms.

Positive		Negative
Probing, questioning		Ignoring
Advising, suggesting		Withdrawing
Praising, agreeing		Name-calling
Reassuring	Listening attentively	Blaming, shaming
Sympathizing		Judging, criticizing
Consoling		Moralizing, preaching
Respecting views		Threatening
Empathy		Warning, admonishing
Supporting		Ordering, directing

We need to explore ways of generating an open, caring, non-threatening classroom climate where pupils feel comfortable about sharing their experiences and ideas.

What techniques are worthwhile in the constant fostering of this type of classroom climate which will help individual pupils develop positive feelings about themselves? Above, a classification of levels of communication has been attempted. Attentiveness in listening is fundamental as a skill for both pupils and teacher. The column labelled POSITIVE signifies increasing levels of warmth in communication, while that labelled NEGATIVE indicates increasing levels of coldness and arbitrary treatment of the individual. By sharing such a model from time to time with staff colleagues in a school, with parents at evening parent-teacher association meetings and with pupils, members of the school community should be able to heighten their understanding of ways in which they can foster values of helping, caring, sharing and concern for others.

Teachers also need to be aware of ways in which 'body talk' and facial expressions can affect interpersonal relations. These range in positive form from smiling, nodding, lifting eyebrows, winking, looking attentively, opening arms, shaking hands and applauding, to the negative responses of frowning, closing eyes slowly, glaring, staring down at pupils, sneering, folding arms, foot tapping, hands on hips, or turning away while a student is talking. The actions of the teacher reveal to pupils how they are regarded and many of us are unaware of our mannerisms in teaching style.

John Buckland, Audrey Jones and Yvonne Duncan (eds.), *Peace Education: The Aotearoa/New Zealand Way*, Auckland, Teaching Resource Centre, Auckland College of Education, 1989.

Developing awareness of their styles of teaching and fundamental stances towards students is essential to perfecting teachers' capacities for maintaining authentically tolerant classrooms. Some readers may want to consult Chapter 2 of Unit 2 on the characteristics of the tolerant classroom.

Values and intercultural education

Because education for tolerance is education for value formation, long a concern for UNESCO, the following guidelines from *A Sense of Belonging: Guidelines for Values for the Humanistic and International Dimensions of Education* (CIDREE/UNESCO, 1993) are useful in clarifying the role of the school in values formation for tolerance.

- Recognize the interactions that take place between cultures.
- Recognize the values of different cultures in a way which does not hide relations of dominance but enhances the status of migrant's cultures.
- Challenge socially-biased and ethnocentric assessment criteria.
- Introduce the intercultural approach in all areas of the organization and life of the school.

- Develop mutual solidarity and acceptance in the living community of the school.
- Recognize and value the symbolic role of the presence of mother tongues in the school.
- Promote a pluralistic approach to the acquisition of knowledge.
- Recognize the potential of the arts for developing an appreciation of different cultures.
- Promote intercultural activity among pupils and recognize that it depends on the quality of co-operation in teaching teams and between indigenous and foreign teachers.
- Promote communications between the schools, the home, the social environment in which the children live and the whole community, both migrant and indigenous.
- Recognize that intercultural education provides a perspective which concerns both the countries of origin and the host countries, and which calls for solidarity between countries with differing levels of resources.
- Develop teacher skills which allow these principles to become effective practice.

A framework for teaching tolerance: social goals and problems

Societies educate to develop values, achieve goals and solve problems. Education is planned so as to provide the knowledge and capacities necessary for learners to exercise pro-social values in their own behaviours and to take action to assure that the policies and arrangements of their societies manifest the same values. The framework for teaching tolerance offered here is thus derived from values, goals and problems or obstacles to the fulfilment of the values and achievement of the goals.

Like any living system, the well-being of human society depends upon the healthy integration of its various parts. Thus tolerance is essential to the healthy integration of the diverse members of human society. However, as living systems also have to be safeguarded against elements that undermine health and well-being, there are conditions that society cannot tolerate.

Table 1 provides a summary of the social goals and obstacles that form the conceptual framework for education for tolerance. Teaching and learning are thus directed towards the achievement of these particular goals of tolerance and overcoming the problems that are major obstacles to the universal realization of human dignity.

Table 1. Tolerance, a conceptual framework: social goals and problems

Value concepts	Goals – tolerance	Problems – intolerance	Processes of tolerance
Peace	Civil disputation; constructive conflict; co-operative social relationships	Violence: physical, structural, cultural, psychological	Peacekeeping and other means of restraining violence and remediating its destructive consequences Negotiation, mediation, adjudication (non-violent conflict resolution)
Human rights	Cultural variety; religious diversity; political pluralism; economic equity; social justice; healthful environment	Sexism, racism, ethnocentrism, poverty, exploitation, prejudice, discrimination, oppression, environmental degradation	Cross-cultural co-operation; interreligious dialogue; human rights protections; equitable resource distribution; sustainable development
Democracy	Multiple political philosophies and opinions; public policy debate; full and openly available information	Impediments to political participation; denial of fundamental freedoms; censorship and manipulation of public information	Fair and open political discussions; representative/participatory decision-making; responsible information media free to inform the public on public issues

A futuristic perspective

Like all forms of education for peace and global citizenship, education for tolerance, with a culture of peace as its general social goal, is often characterized by a futuristic perspective consistent with the framework proposed here.

The United Nations Children's Fund (UNICEF) Middle East and North African Regional Office, in association with the ministries of education, has undertaken the development of futuristic global education curricula and teaching strategies in the same spirit of holistic, values-oriented approach as advocated in UNESCO's Integrated framework of Action for Education for peace, human rights and democracy.

Global education is a future-oriented concept of education which promotes the notion that the classroom environment should focus on knowledge, skills, values and attitudes that children will need in the complex, rapidly changing and interdependent world of tomorrow. This notion argues: that the educational process should foster an awareness and understanding of the increasingly integrated nature of the contemporary world; that contemporary global issues, such as environmental degradation, human rights denial, conflict and world inequalities are interlocking, and can create conflict between groups with different values and perspectives; and that the future needs to be brought centrally into the educational process so that students are given the opportunity to study, reflect upon and discuss probable, possible and preferred futures.

S. V. Hitachi and Frank Dall, *Situation Report on the Global Education Project in MENA, Amman,* UNICEF/MENARO, 17 January 1995.

General learning goals: values, knowledge and skills

The learning goals of education for tolerance are broad and comprehensive, encompassing a range of content and skills in the context of the value of human dignity and the values that have been described here as deriving from tolerance.

The knowledge essential to the practice of tolerance is determined by the values sought. Much of the substantive content that would form the fundamental knowledge base has been suggested in Chapter 2 where the forms, indicators and signs of intolerance and tolerance were outlined. That material can serve as a base for presenting and acquiring data and information on the goals and obstacles that affect peace, human rights and democracy.

The skills development sought is directed towards providing learners with capacities to deal constructively with all types of human differences, political controversies and social conflicts. In stating such general learning goals, it is helpful to include a kind of summary statement, in broad terms, of what those who are to practise tolerance should value, know and be able to do. Such a summary appears in Table 2, illustrating the relationships between the three categories of learning goals.

Education for tolerance is most appropriately assessed on the basis of the learners' performance of the skills required to exercise tolerance, so some performance objectives are included.

Table 2. Tolerance: general learning goals

Values	Knowledge	Capacities and skills	Basis for assessment
Human dignity (human rights)	Varieties of human, personal and cultural identities, social issues	**Living with diversity** Cross-cultural co-operation; using human rights standards to make judgements	Performance in actual cross-cultural tasks; performance in applying human rights standards to cases of violation
Social justice (democracy)	Multiple forms of democratic processes and governance	**Exercising responsibility** Critical reflection; communication of facts and opinions; political decision-making	Presentation of interpretation of sample situations; presentation of description of problems and potential solutions; presentation of reasons for a political position
Co-operative non-violent society (peace)	Alternative ways of responding constructively to human differences and conflicts	**Managing conflict** Discussion and debate; conflict resolution; reconciliation; social reconstruction; co-operative problem-solving and task achievement	Oral and written arguments describing alternatives, choosing one, and stating reasons for choice; simulation of conflict-resolution procedures and approaches to reconciliation

REALMS OF LEARNING: A PROCESS FOR TEACHING TOLERANCE

Tolerance, as we have seen, is the threshold value for reversing processes of intolerance and violence. In seeking to educate for tolerance, it is helpful to visualize the process of education in terms of realms of learning experience that comprise a lifelong learning process towards a culture of peace.

Planning educational experiences to help learners enter these realms can be described in terms of human qualities and capacities. Here, tolerance is seen both as a threshold value or condition of peace-building and as an expanding capacity to make and build peace. If tolerance is to be an opening to a wider process of education for peace, human rights and democracy, the realms of tolerance must be continually broadened. This broadening is always tempered by the core values of human dignity and integrity, with limits to tolerance emerging when these core values are violated. Thus, the following realms of learning comprise a process of teaching for tolerance. The suggestions and examples of instructional procedures described in the curriculum supplements (Units 2 and 3) and the projects reported in Chapters 5 and 6 of this core unit serve as vehicles for entering these realms of learning.

Tolerance ➡ Acknowledgement of others' rights to life and to dignity.

Acquaintance ➡ Welcoming awareness of the presence of others in one's social sphere.

Respect for differences ➡ Acknowledgement of the positive aspects of diversity.

Understanding of uniqueness ➡ Appreciation of particular forms of human diversity.

Complementarity as the principle of relating to difference ➡ Capacity to integrate differences so as to enrich and strengthen society.

Mutuality as basis for co-operative endeavours ➡ Capacity to envision and work towards common goals that are mutually advantageous to diverse groups.

A culture of peace ➡ Recognition of interdependence and human universals, and undertaking to work towards positive arrangements of diversity in an interdependent world, comprised of convivial communities.

FOR STUDY AND DISCUSSION: STARTING A PROCESS OF LEARNING TOLERANCE

▶ How might the framework presented here be adapted to the particular conditions of your community and classes?

▶ What opportunities are there in your school(s) for co-operative learning and training in conflict resolution? Have your teachers been trained in these methods?

▶ What issues and concerns in the area of human rights education are most appropriate for study in your school(s) and community(ies)?

▶ How can your class or group assess readiness for study and activity in the various realms of learning that make up the process of learning towards a culture of peace? In what ways can you expand learning and practice beyond the threshold value of tolerance?

Review the programmes, projects and approaches listed in Chapter 5 and the selections in the curriculum supplements to see if some are appropriate as models for a process of learning tolerance in your own school(s).

Objectives of the process for teaching tolerance

The particular objectives that would be espoused by teachers engaged in the process for teaching tolerance are articulated and enumerated in the basic objectives of a unit on tolerance prepared for the International Year of Tolerance by the Permanent Seminar on Education for Peace, Galicia, Spain.

1. Develop awareness about causes of violence and intolerance within a spirit of co-operation and peace.
2. Promote an education based on tolerance and respect for others, especially those most marginalized in today's society.
3. Encourage the practice of tolerance as a means to maintaining peace, justice and respect for human rights.
4. Strengthen communication and freedom of expression in the struggle against all forms of discrimination and marginalization, and develop the conviction that tolerance is best manifested in the respect for the dignity of persons and in political freedom.
5. Prepare students to live in a changing, multicultural society which demands an attitude of tolerance and acceptance of different cultures that struggles against inhuman and degrading treatment and respect for human persons without distinction in regard to sex, age, race, language, religion, political opinions, national or social origin.
6. Contribute to the development of peace, solidarity, and international understanding and co-operation.
7. Denounce the simplistic and dogmatic views of fanaticism and integralism of all kinds; give support in a critical spirit in favour of conviviality and tolerance as most conducive to understanding among persons and peoples.
8. Establish (in classrooms) habits and attitudes for resolving problems in creative and dialogic ways, involving the values of peace, justice, solidarity, co-operation and tolerance in our daily lives.
9. Teach students the necessity of renouncing violence and adopting peaceful methods to resolve problems and conflicts.
10. Inspire in the present generation of students – who will hold future positions of responsibility – sentiments of altruism, openness, respect for others, solidarity and participation based on their own identities and the capacity to recognize that there are many ways to be human in different cultural and social contexts.

From *Sobre Tolerancia*, Unidade No. 11, Semenario Permanente de Educación para la Paz.

The teacher: the heart of the educational process

Schools are only as good as their teachers. The teacher is the very heart of the educational process. The professional competence and personal capacities of the teacher will determine the success of any curriculum. In educating for tolerance, the preparation of the teacher is crucial. Special efforts to prepare teachers for their crucial role in education for tolerance, human rights, democracy and peace have been advocated by UNESCO, ministries and agencies dedicated to such education. For example, educators for peace in New Zealand have proposed the following guidelines for the role of the teacher:

The teacher of peace and tolerance

- appreciates his/her impact as a role model;
- acquires and uses appropriate skills to promote peaceful relationships and resolve conflicts;
- encourages creative responses to problem-solving;
- provides co-operative and challenging activities which encourage initiative and personal achievement rather than aggressive or highly competitive behaviour;
- encourages student and parent participation in decision-making and in planning programmes;
- draws on community resources in the development of learning programmes and is sensitive to community needs and perceptions;
- requires critical thinking and appreciation of other viewpoints while remaining alert to his or her own position on controversial issues;
- values cultural diversity by providing opportunities to understand and experience cultural differences.

Adapted from John Buckland, Audrey Jones and Yvonne Duncan (eds.), *Peace Education: The Aotearoa/New Zealand Way*, Auckland, Teaching Resource Centre, Auckland College of Education, 1989.

The training of teachers, especially the pre-service preparation through which young professionals are given their vision of the role and responsibilities of the teaching profession, must take into account the need to nurture the attributes the New Zealand peace educators designated as those of the authentic and effective teacher of peace and tolerance. A similar view emanating from this is expressed by Dr Ana Cecilia Manrique of the Permanent Delegation of Colombia to UNESCO, who suggests the following as the basic principles for a teacher-training programme for a culture of peace.

The following points are considered the most important and may constitute the basic principles of a teacher-training programme for a culture of peace:

- Educating in and for love.
- Projecting and reflecting peace.
- Involving parents and the community.
- Encouraging participation.
- Respecting individual importance and ability, together with feelings and viewpoints.
- Creating a moral sense of justice.
- Less rigidly hierarchical relations.
- Democracy in class and training in freedom.
- Dispelling authoritarianism and manipulation.
- Dialogue, understanding and solidarity.
- Teaching to share.
- Being an example for children and the community. Showing that peace is a real possibility.
- Fostering tolerance and sincerity.
- Knowing how to listen.
- Liking what is done.
- Asserting the value of affective ties and guiding pupils' affectivity.
- Letting pupils resolve problems.

Blanca Navas de Iriarte, *Una Cultura de Paz a Traves de la Educación*, p. 10, Sante Fe de Bogota, July 1994. (Paper prepared for UNESCO Culture of Peace Programme.)

And from Asia too, the same fundamental concepts are put forth, emphasizing the need to develop skills for teaching with participatory methods and focusing on value-based problems.

The Workshop affirmed pedagogical concerns, noting particularly the call for activities such as role-playing, appeals to empathy, modelling of key principles, a deliberate and consistent application of these stages of moral development.

It is recommended that goals of staff development should include a future perspective emphasizing the promotion of international understanding, social justice, human rights and ecological sustainability; the understanding of world problems, their effects on the survival and well-being of humankind, and the responsibility towards their reduction; and the appreciation of cultural diversities, indigenous cultures and cultural heritages.

UNESCO Regional Workshop on International Education Materials and Methods, Bandung, Indonesia, 3–7 August 1993.

We refer to the teacher as the heart of the educational process for two fundamental reasons. First, it is the teacher who gives life to the experiences that make it possible for students to learn. Equally significant, it is the teacher's values, attitudes, knowledge and skills that determine the climate and the results of what happens in the classroom. As the heart provides the fundamental energies of life for the human body, the teacher provides the energies for learning values and relationships to students. The teaching of peace and tolerance depends upon a tolerant and peaceful classroom, and such classrooms are created by tolerant and peaceful teachers.

Teachers, however, are human beings subject to the same influences and socialization processes as members of any community. While families and cultural groups may have somewhat differing values and attitudes, it is unlikely that most people in any society that suffers from intolerance will *not* be affected by it. Often these effects are not consciously experienced. Nonetheless, they must be identified and faced. An intolerant teacher is unable to educate for tolerance. So it is best to face these problems in the preparatory stages before teachers take up their classroom responsibilities.

It is very useful for pre-service and in-service teachers, indeed for all group leaders and those who are responsible for guiding and facilitating the learning of others, to be aware of their own levels of tolerance and, in this world of diversity, to be able to assess their own understanding of others, who differ from them in any manner. The World Association of Girl Guides and Girl Scouts offers an excellent tool for just that purpose. The following questionnaire is taken from their module on *Cultural Understanding*, a useful resource for schools or communities seeking to undertake education for tolerance, particularly as it applies to cross-cultural, multicultural and intercultural relations. It is an especially useful tool for use in teacher-education classes, training prospective educators to teach for cross-cultural understanding.

Your community and country

Who are the people in your community? How do they live, work, and enjoy life within the community? What do they believe? The following brief assessment will help you determine what you already know or need to know about people in your community.

Learning experience

Indicate the level of your knowledge by checking the appropriate rating for each knowledge area.

Your community			
Knowledge areas	Your level (rating)		
	Absent	Low	Medium	High
Languages	O	O	O	O
Foods	O	O	O	O
Arts	O	O	O	O
Racial-ethnic groups	O	O	O	O
Education	O	O	O	O
Values	O	O	O	O
Social customs	O	O	O	O
Religions	O	O	O	O
Non-verbal expressions	O	O	O	O
History	O	O	O	O

What areas do you consider areas of strength? ....

Where do you need to learn more? ....

Comments: ....

World Association of Girl Guides and Girl Scouts (WAGGS), *Cultural and International Understanding.*

The content of teacher education

From the Russian Federation come these suggestions for the content of teacher education that add substance to the values concerns of the Colombian and New Zealand suggestions, and reflect the principles of integration and holism that are articulated in UNESCO's Integrated Framework of Action on Education for Peace, Human Rights and Democracy.

Priorities of contemporary education

An outline of a course for education departments, universities and colleges for pre-service and in-service teacher education

1. General approaches
- This course can be presented as a course in itself or as a special topic integrated into other education courses.
- It is based on the documents of UNESCO and other international organizations dealing with global developments and requirements for education at the end of the twentieth and beginning of the twenty-first century.
- The course is intended as a realization of the principles of the Project on Ecological and Co-operative Education (established in 1988,

involving educators from Norway, the Russian Federation, Ukraine and the United States).

2. Course objectives

The students will acquire:

* an orientation towards the new paradigm of education which derives from the holistic thinking required by global problems of security, ecology, conflict, etc.;
* a system of knowledge about educational aims and methodology needed for solving global problems;
* practical skills for communication developed for contemporary education.

3. Key ideas of the course

The course is based on five key sets of ideas:

* a holistic and critical worldview within a framework of a sustainable, inclusive world order;
* global priorities and global, local and personal security;
* ecology, non-violence, human rights, rights of the child;
* new economic order, new economy, democratization;
* social responsibility, social activity, multicultural education;
* global ethics and co-operation.

4. The structure of the course includes:

* lectures;
* seminars;
* workshops.

[This core conceptual resource would be a useful text for the lectures and seminars. Units 2 and 3 for elementary and secondary schools would be useful for the workshops.]

5. Curriculum

* Lectures to provide content and background:
    – the world as a single integrated system; nature, humankind, individual, global problems. The need for the new paradigm;
    – education for living in an integrated world;
    – education for ecological security;
    – education for economic and social security;
    – education for personal security;
    – a co-operative world through co-operative education.
* Seminars to clarify the key ideas, principles and values:
    – the idea of holism. History of modern views;
    – non-violence as a basic principle of the relationship between human beings and between human beings and nature;
    – human rights and tolerance.

- Workshops to train students in practical teaching skills:
  - peaceful conflict resolution;
  - mutual understanding;
  - communication and co-operation.
- Practical activities: students are involved in such co-operative activities as planting greenery and organizing public services in the community, on students' campuses and in schools to demonstrate active and participatory education for social responsibility.

Valentina Mitina and Emilia Sokolova (educators for peace and mutual understanding, Russian Federation), *Ecological and Co-operative Education in Teacher Training* (Peace Education Reports, No. 12, August 1994).

Human rights violations as content of teacher education

As indicated earlier, authentic tolerance requires the observance of limits. Too often these limits have been stretched too far and the intolerable becomes the unconscionable, the shame of society. Intolerance has, in fact, contributed to crimes of such dimensions that they have been designated as crimes against humanity, genocide, apartheid and torture as well as rape and severe abuse of women and children. Teachers need to be able to communicate to their students the consequences of intolerance in terms of actual human experience and suffering. Feature films are an excellent instructional device for this purpose. To fully explore and understand the experiences, more maturity and some knowledge of the historical cases is required. Suggested here for teacher education, this approach is also recommended for upper-secondary level and colleges. The following syllabus was adapted from one devised by Yasuyo Fukunaga, a teacher of English in Japan. The approach, however, has also been used in social studies and as a supplement in literature classes. Films on similar themes exist in various languages, many of them on video easily adaptable to classroom use in schools with monitors and VCR players. A selected list of such films appears in the Appendices.

The cases and events depicted show some human consequences of intolerance which can be assessed as violations of human rights. Thus, the relevant international standards should be included among the readings. Teachers and teacher educators adapting this syllabus should begin with a reading of the Universal Declaration of Human Rights, the violations of which are indicators of the intolerable.

Crimes of intolerance: the human experience of rights violations

1. *The Killing Fields*
   Topics: Politicide, genocide and refugees
   Read: International Convention on Genocide, International Convention on the Rights of Refugees.

2. *Schindler's List*
   Topics: Genocide, the Holocaust and concentration camps
   Read: Nuremberg Principles.

3. *Mississippi Burning*
   Topic: Racism and the civil rights movement in the United States
   Read: International Convention on the Elimination of All Forms of Racial Discrimination.

4. *The Color Purple*
   Topic: Sexism and child abuse
   Read: International Convention on the Elimination of All Forms of Discrimination against Women and/or the Convention on the Rights of the Child.

5. *The Mission*
   Topic: Indigenous people, genocide and colonialism
   Read: Draft Convention on the Rights of Indigenous Peoples.

6. *Cry Freedom*
   Topic: Apartheid
   Read: International Convention on the Suppression and Punishment of the Crime of Apartheid, African Freedom Charter.

FOR STUDY AND DISCUSSION: ADDRESSING THE PROBLEMS

▶ Reflect on the relationship between tolerance and peace. What do you consider to be the most damaging forms of violence in the world? Does your community suffer from violence? In what forms? Are non-violent alternatives available?

▶ What do you believe to be the most serious human-rights abuses in the world? Do you know of any efforts to remedy them? Are there human-rights problems and issues in your community? How are they being addressed?

▶ What are the most serious impediments to democracy? How might the world community address any one of these impediments? How could your own community participate in that process?

- What is the significance of a futuristic perspective to young learners?
- How should issues of tolerance, human rights and peace be integrated into the content of teacher education? What is the importance of global and futuristic perspectives?
- What qualities and capacities for effective teaching shoud be emphasized in preparing teachers to educate for tolerance?

5. Suggestions for teaching tolerance

The first four chapters of this resource have provided a rationale, framework and context for education for tolerance at all levels and in all spheres of education, with some emphasis on schools. This chapter deals with school-based practice, offering a few brief suggestions on where to integrate education for tolerance into school curricula and some examples of how many schools and education systems are approaching this vital sphere in the preparation of a culture of peace. The purpose of this chapter is simply to point out the range of possibilities, not to describe teaching approaches in replicable detail (some are presented in the two curriculum units). Many more possibilities exist and UNESCO hopes that users of this resource will continue to share their ideas and experiences for the continued improvement and expansion of education for peace, human rights and democracy.

Infusion: tolerance in all disciplines

Tolerance, like all other aspects of education for peace, human rights and democracy, can and should be brought into the schools through two fundamental approaches – first, through explicit instruction designed to achieve the intended learning goals and, second, through infusion of the themes, ethics and behaviour patterns of tolerance throughout the schooling experience. Every subject area and activity offers possibilities for communicating to students the concepts, values and practices that tolerance contributes to the formation of communities. The school is itself both a community and a learning laboratory for participation in the wider communities at local, national and global levels.

Language education: a vehicle for cross-cultural learning

The learning of languages is one of the most fruitful avenues for education for tolerance and mutual understanding. Indeed, only in the mastery of its language can another culture be understood fully and truly. Study of language involving study of the history and culture of a people offers opportunities for lessons in some of the following topics:

- cultural values and the experiences and events that have influenced their formation;
- social customs and institutions, viewed in comparative terms that illustrate the different ways in which human universals such as family structure, celebrations, occasions of mourning and so forth are expressed;
- reading aloud poetry, epics or the words of national anthems as a basis for reflection on how a people has responded to its common experience.

Literature: a means for the study of values

Literature from other cultures, even in translation, provides a basis for understanding the values and experience of others in terms more lively and human than the study of their political histories abstracted from the social experiences of a people. Some of many useful practices to teach towards tolerance in literature would include the following:

- in teaching about any national epic include at least extracts and résumés of those of one or two other cultures to demonstrate how this art form is common;
- children's stories and nursery rhymes from various cultures could be included in the curricula of kindergarten and nursery schools;
- primary schools could study how various cultures celebrate and honour their heroes in stories that recount the virtues and contributions of these heroes;
- secondary schools could introduce courses in multicultural literature to teach young people the works of the great writers of various cultures, indicating which were contemporary with their own great writers.

The great works of various religions should also be the bases of courses designed to educate for tolerance.

History: towards an inclusive view of the human experience

The teaching of history has often been a factor in developing attitudes of hostility, exclusion and prejudice towards others. Most national histories, having been presented to a people from their own perspective, have given little or no attention to how events may have appeared to other groups. Often the experiences of women and minorities have not been recounted. In most histories, more attention has been given to war and conflict than to peace and co-operation. Thus, in educating for tolerance, special measures must be taken to revise and supplement standard histories. Some of the possibilities for doing so are listed below:

• students carry out research concerning proposals for peace that may have been made to prevent the wars recounted in their texts;

• students themselves speculate on steps that might have been taken to avoid wars and other outbreaks of violence;

• classes co-operate in writing a 'history of the future' recounting how the plague of intolerance was 'cured through education for tolerance' and how the coming of tolerance led to peace;

• students from minority groups share family stories of events recounted by their grandparents and parents as a way of contributing another dimension to the official record;

• teachers show films from other countries depicting historical events from different perspectives;

• students research and 'imagine' events from the perspectives of those whose stories are not told, such as indigenous people, women and ethnic groups who have been destroyed or assimilated out of their own cultures;

• re-enact, using role-play techniques, great moments in history in order to gain insight into whether decisions were made from a basis of tolerance or intolerance.

Social studies and civics: learning the norms of tolerance

In those subjects that form the content basis of education for citizenship, education for tolerance should include some study of the international human-rights standards, the possibilities for their implementation and the obstacles to their realization. There are a very wide variety of teaching practices for these purposes. Among the most readily adaptable are the following:

Post a copy of the Universal Declaration of Human Rights and the Convention on the Rights of the Child in every classroom. In primary-level classrooms, one of the several simplified versions of these documents could be used. Discuss one article of one or both documents each day or week throughout the school term.

Use concepts and standards of human rights as the basis for formulating class rules.

Have the social studies and/or civics class prepare a special assembly for Human Rights Day, 10 December.

Study the Declaration of Principles on Tolerance (see Appendix 3) and the conditions which led to its drafting. Discuss the situations in the world today which led to the United Nations addressing the issue anew. What could be done to try to bring tolerance to the areas of the world torn by intolerance and intergroup strife?

Study what the United Nations, UNESCO and non-governmental organizations can do to protect human rights. Discuss what the students themselves can do. Undertake human-rights learning actions such as letter-writing and participating in organizational efforts on behalf of human rights.

The sciences: questions of ethics and responsibilities

Education for tolerance in the sciences at the secondary-school level provides an appropriate basis for introducing and exploring issues related to the responsibilities that go with knowledge. As students learn the history of the twentieth century, they will discover that the sciences have been used to serve the ends of intolerance as well as the relief of suffering and injustice. As they acquire scientific knowledge, they will be called upon to make choices concerning how to use their knowledge. The suggestions here relate to raising questions of ethics and responsibility.

In physics courses, some of the following issues could be raised:

- the ethical implications of the use of physics for the development of weapons of mass destruction or for the construction of the means to carry out genocide or inflict torture;
- the content and significance of 'statements of conscience' made by physicists.

In courses in the natural sciences, some of the following topics could be addressed:

- the ways in which natural systems adjust and accommodate to change and to the introduction of new or 'foreign' elements;
- the principles of symbiosis and how some life-forms develop modes of co-existence and mutual interdependence;

- the Seville Statement on Violence (UNESCO, 1992), which challenges theories of human aggression, as the basis for the development of tolerance as the social norm and the evolution of a culture of peace.

Mathematics: the statistics of equity

Tolerance as a positive value calls for economic equity and distributive justice. The realization of these two tolerance-related values requires knowledge and understanding of quantities of resources and of how they are used, distributed and shared. Some of the following activities could help learners to understand the value implications of economic structures and patterns:

Using literacy statistics, especially as they relate to differences between men and women, and between the nations of the North and South to illustrate patterns of educational advantages and disadvantages.

Using comparative figures on arms and social expenditure to calculate the percentage of the world's wealth that is spent for purposes of violent conflict.

The arts: articulating human universals

The arts are probably the most promising of all subject areas for educating for tolerance; they are the medium through which universal human aspirations are most vividly expressed. Teaching both the appreciation and the performance of the arts can provide opportunities for the following and many other approaches:

- in art history courses, examples of works of the same period from other cultures should be included. Painting, sculpture, etc., should be reviewed in terms of universal human themes and how they are expressed from culture to culture;

- folk arts could be studied as ways to learn the values, and the aesthetic and design senses of various cultures;

- works of art could be used to judge the state of tolerance in a society in terms of images of 'others', both minorities within countries and others from distant places;

- popular arts and media could be reviewed for instances of stereotypes, racism, sexism, denigration and defamation of others. Cartoons just before or during wars and cultural clashes could be studied to learn how popular art has been used to fan the flames of intolerance;

- in practical arts classes, themes related to tolerance, human rights and peace could be assigned as subjects for drawings, paintings or making school posters;
- children could do drawings of *The Garden of Human Diversity,* showing different faces as a wonderful panoply of human beings;
- the music of human-rights movements and ethnic groups could be played, sung and discussed to learn the values and goals of ethnic and other groups who struggle for tolerance and human rights. Students could discuss how music and art provide inspiration and energy to such endeavours;
- students could compose and perform their own music for tolerance, human rights and peace.

A panoply of possibilities: tolerance education as a global movement

Everywhere in the world, even in societies where conflict has broken out into violence, there are those who want to make peace and develop tolerance. What follows are brief descriptions of a few of the efforts of such people offered as examples of actions others might also take.

INTERRELIGIOUS UNDERSTANDING

A number of groups throughout the world have addressed the need for education about the various religions of any nation in order to increase understanding and overcome the intolerance born of ignorance. One example is the extensive programme to teach about Islam in the United Kingdom, undertaken by Amana, a non-governmental organization.

COMMON SCHOOLING AND ENCOUNTERS OF GROUPS IN CONFLICT

In deeply divided societies, the desire for change nearly always comes from the grass roots. Such is the case with much of 'Education for Mutual Understanding' in Northern Ireland and similar efforts in Israel, South Africa and other countries.

Firstly, we shall consider the school whose whole philosophy and structure is directed to the creation of tolerance. In different parts of the world, these schools are variously known as 'co-educational', 'inter-denominational', 'mixed race', 'integrated' and 'comprehensive'. In some cases, they follow particular educational philosophies based on peace and tolerance, such as Waldorf or Steiner Schools. Whatever the name, their goals are the same – to teach children from different communities together on a basis of equality by having the governors, teaching staff, student body and curriculum reflect each community with equal weight.

Sometimes it has not been possible to create schools in this way. Then, 'contact schemes' provide an important opportunity for children to discover and explore new relationships under the guidance of experienced counsellors who understand the aspirations and fears of all those involved in the processes of reconciliation through education for tolerance. Shared holidays, summer camps and specialized retreats are but some of the venues at which positive social change can be carefully nurtured.

The element common to these approaches to education for tolerance is the need for formal education and associated teaching materials, such as those described in the curriculum supplements. These can be used in conjunction with a mixed school or in preparation for a contact event.

In the real world, with all its complexities, a combination of these approaches will be used with various degrees of success and failure. In too many cases, these minority efforts are still frustrated by extreme sectarianism and conflictual social climates. However, as reported below, communities do try.

An experience of reconciliation

The Novalis Institute which trains South African teachers in the methods of the Waldorf schools offers this experience of preparing teachers to contribute to the healing and reconstruction of the racist past of their country. Its report states:

> The apartheid system in South Africa has been most successful in keeping the realities of different communities in the country apart. The Novalis Institute has been most successful in bringing these realities together and facilitating the development of a new reality and consciousness. . . . The shift in consciousness and perceptions of individuals and groups who were privileged to participate in the process facilitated by the Novalis Institute has . . . been the most important and valuable outcome that could possibly have been achieved. It has prepared the way and laid the foundations for a new and integrated [community].

Civic education for a multi-cultural society

In Israel, a Department for Democracy and Coexistence has been established. It publicizes guidelines and assists in the development of educational programmes and projects throughout the country, emphasizing in-service teacher training. The programmes for children rely heavily on the arts and on practice of the skills of participation in a democratic society, especially discussion and debate of controversial issues. Towards this latter end, it encourages instituting democratic practices in schools and, very important to the development of tolerance, 'stresses the importance of verbal civility. . . . It acknowledges the need for the nurturing of the cultural identity of both Arab-Israeli students and Jewish-Israeli students towards promoting a multi-cultural society' (information booklet of the department).

ACTION FOR OUR COMMON FUTURE
MULTI-CULTURAL EDUCATION

The Friedrich-Ebert Foundation in Namibia has produced a mixed media package in six indigenous languages. The package defines tolerance as 'collective action and concern for our common future'. A second Namibian project comes from the Ministry of Education. The Cross Curricular Culture Project seeks to enrich the curriculum with the Namibian culture, 'rich in diversity'. Ten pilot schools throughout the country are working together with their surrounding communities to strengthen cultural aspects, especially in vocational training and the arts. Many creative projects have been devised out of ideas proposed by students. Among the learning objectives for tolerance that are projected for teachers and students are: (a) to see values in and care for nature; (b) to value the work that the elderly do and have done, i.e. their own history; and (c) to learn to know and respect their surrounding community and various styles of life, not just Western consumerism.

SHARING SPACE AND PURPOSE

A UNESCO Associated School in Slovenia has devised a model programme for Slovene and Bosnian children at elementary level. The model comprises the basic elements necessary for such endeavours – the support of the community, the involvement of the parents, the preparation of the teachers and the development of materials. This model could be adapted by many communities, whether in conditions of violence, impending- or post-conflict situations, or by hosts to refugees of different cultures. The following is an excerpt from this programme:

> The Programme will foster among all participants, the community, parents, teachers and students, learning intended to:
> • provide knowledge of human rights as outlined in the international standards promulgated by the United Nations;

- strengthen or change opinions on and persuasions about values of peace, tolerance in mutual relations, and rights of every human being;
- strengthen or change attitudes and actual behaviour towards others so that there will be more tolerant co-operation and inclination towards mutual help.

A SURVEY ON VIOLENCE

In Colombia, a country that has known violence of many kinds over the centuries and in recent years suffered a conflict between the government and the drug traffickers, violence has become the focus of a programme for the construction of a culture of peace. Carried out through the Associated Schools with the support and co-operation of the Ministry of Education, this programme researched the concepts of violence and peace held by thousands of young people throughout the country; it reflected on how these young people see their society and in what terms they envision one that is more peaceful and tolerant. Such a project would be a useful initial step for many communities intending to initiate programmes of education for tolerance.

EXTRA-CURRICULAR ACTIVITIES

Among the European countries where educators are responding to the challenges of multiculturalism, France has been especially active in the extra-curricular area, encouraging encounters between adolescents of different cultures, thereby providing opportunities for open discussions to help the young understand differences and see them in a complementary relationship. Some schools have established human-rights clubs.

The Resonant Community programme in Norway brings children of many ethnic groups together for musical performances in order to overcome prejudice and racism. The Council of Europe encourages similar activities. A major effort on Foreigners in Our Town has involved individuals of all ages in Germany to combat prejudice.

CELEBRATING THE POTENTIAL OF YOUTH

The celebration of human identity is found in virtually all cultures. Celebration, indeed, is a mode for sharing those aspects of cultural identity that mark human communities. Cultural festivals of all sorts are a very effective approach to intercultural understanding within and across international borders. Excellent results were achieved by the 1993 International

Festival of the Youth of Chad, a co-operative effort of the Ministry of Education and the National Commission for UNESCO.

This festival brought together youth from various ethnic and tribal groups to launch a cultural-revalorization campaign through which they were able to share cultural traditions as contributions to their shared collective community. The core values articulated by the various delegations made evident the possibility of a mutually enhancing relationship between cultures: active solidarity as the mode of accepting others, dialogue as a means of breaking down the barriers of hatred that separate one people from another and respect of the other as a basis of mutual understanding and peace.

The importance of youth as the major population group of Africa and the world, and as a source of human potential for leadership and responsibility, was acknowledged by the festival.

INTERNATIONAL AND MULTI-CULTURAL EDUCATION

In 1991, the Sainte-Marie de Hann School in Senegal, a UNESCO Associated School, was awarded the UNESCO Prize for Peace Education. The school has 4,000 pupils, boys and girls of forty-eight different nationalities, from kindergarten to secondary level. Its activities include building within the school a House of Cultures with travelling exhibitions, meetings with artists to promote the discovery of diverse cultures among young people and creating a 'rainbow' foundation to encourage and stimulate the various initiatives for international understanding in Senegal.

ACKNOWLEDGING BICULTURALISM

In some countries where indigenous cultures have not been honoured and indigenous people's concerns and contributions have not been reflected in the curriculum, ministries of education are now making efforts to rectify this injustice. An example of such an effort is the inclusion of Maori language and culture in the *New Zealand Syllabus for Junior Classes of Form 2* which emphasizes biculturalism. It reflects an appreciation of the importance of language or cultural integrity and a sense of human dignity. According to the syllabus, 'Respect for other people, provision of equity for all, and acknowledgement of differences are marks of a mature and tolerant society. . . . A society, in which all people are respected for what they are, requires an understanding of other cultures.'

Similar efforts are being made with indigenous languages in other countries. Brazil, for example, is conducting a literacy programme in the Ticun language. Study of the cultures and problems of indigenous people in many nations has become a major effort of education for tolerance in all areas. Notably, Canadian and American educators are developing materials and programmes to teach about the many cultures of the First Americans. Costa Rica's Associated Schools have conducted an intensive programme on the cultures of the country's various indigenous people.

TEACHER TRAINING FOR GLOBAL CITIZENSHIP

Three fundamental themes of tolerance were integrated into teacher education by the Peace and World Order Studies Program (PWOS) of the Philippine Normal University.

Modules for intercultural awareness, gender sensitivity and human-rights education were developed to assist teachers to carry out the goals of PWOS. Students preparing for teaching were trained to conduct workshops that develop group sensitivity and promote respect for human rights, gender equality and intercultural understanding.

PWOS is in line with the university's goals to promote progressive leadership in education responsive to the needs and requirements of the twenty-first century. PWOS is itself a form of political citizenship education which is global in outlook, human-value-centred, problem-solving and futuristic. Its primary concerns are peace, education for democracy, human rights and gender equality, ecological balance and intercultural understanding. The task PWOS has undertaken is to develop specific approaches and methodologies for teaching these peace and global values and concepts, either as a separate course or integrated into existing courses.

CORRESPONDENCE IN IMAGES: SCHOOL TWINNING

The art-education teachers of the federal secondary academic school, Parhamerplatz, Vienna, and the Kralovo Pole secondary school in Brno (Czech Republic), stimulated by a school twinning scheme and co-operation arrangements between the headmasters, developed a project which, through art, was designed to overcome barriers and see the 'other' as an extension of the self. The teachers from both schools together designed a concept for the project which provided for the exchange of semi-finished student works (pictures and objects focusing on the tolerance theme) which were then finished by the respective partner in the neighbouring country. In this way, joint border-crossing works of art were created. The students and teachers visited each other. The impetus coming from outside had a highly stimulating effect on the students in both schools; the foreign language awoke curiosity and there was no element of competition. The works created in the course of the project were exhibited to the public. The very successful *vernissage* was held in Vienna, and students from the Czech Republic attended; it involved a performance consisting of movements and texts in a language foreign to everybody involved – Latin.

TOGETHERNESS TOWARDS COMMUNITY: A SMALL RURAL TOWN

In the course of discussing the concept of 'tolerance' at the federal secondary academic school at Rohrbach (Austria), the idea of leaving the school boundaries to stage an activity in the main square of Rohrbach so as to attract more attention to the subject was born. In the preparatory stage, a banner was made inscribed with the motto: 'TOLERANCE – Let's regard each other/Let's talk to each other'. Participants also prepared and copied folded leaflets with symbolic depictions of otherness (pairs of shoes of different sizes and from different cultures, with their owners pictured on the reverse). The activity itself consisted of some students singing songs in front of the banner, while others distributed the leaflets and tried to enter into discussions with passers-by based on questionnaires on the subject of 'tolerance–intolerance'. In the follow-up phase, the responses to the questionnaires were analysed and the students considered their own attitudes.

'SALUT L'ÉTRANGER!': INTERCULTURAL DAYS

The objective of 'Salut l'Étranger!', organized by the Communauté Neuchâteloise de Travail pour l'Intégration Sociale des Étrangers (CNTISE), is to improve relations between the native Swiss and foreign residents in the canton of Neuchâtel.

The programme consisted of various events such as food, film, dance and theatre festivals where different countries were represented. Schools organized open days, and some cultural centres and other organizations opened their doors as well. A number of conferences were organized on topics such as European culture and religions, the Western world and the Arabic world, and cultural-pluralism and nationalism in Europe.

By organizing these intercultural days, 'Salut l'Étranger!' is not only promoting tolerance and solidarity among people from different countries, but also underlining the multiculturalism of the canton as a community resource.

RECLAIMING CROSS-CULTURAL SOLIDARITY

Sri Lanka has lived for ten years with the struggle between the majority Sinhalese community and the Tamil minority. Linguistic and religious differences have enhanced an ethnic division between the two communities and the young people of the present generation are almost totally unaware of the historically peaceful and friendly co-existence that their parents enjoyed in the past.

A cultural programme consists of a collaborative exercise between two schools, each from a different community, presenting their traditional folk dances in a one-to-one sequence. The programme demonstrates that the values, feelings, emotions and forms of expression cherished and practised by both communities are no different one from the other. Steps are being taken to extend this style of multi-ethnic cultural presentation in schools to other districts.

CORDIAL COMMUNICATIONS AND LANGUAGE FOR PEACE

Osnovna skola 'Tin Ujevic', a primary school in Croatia, held a three-day seminar entitled 'Language of a Snake and a Giraffe', aimed at reducing barriers in human conversation and based on the concept of 'warm' and 'cold' language. The idea was to overcome the hostile, cold and rational language dominant in our everyday life and society. The language of a snake can be polite, but very cold, formal and rational, creating barriers in human relationships, while the language of a giraffe – a warm language – is full of emotion and understanding. It brings human emotions and desires to the surface, helps people get to know each other better and understand one another's motives and actions. Warm language helps us to become more human and build a society that avoids violent conflicts and the hostilities that ruin our lives and threaten our planet.

Another language project, LINGUAPAX, is a UNESCO project which aims at promoting teaching of languages and literature in order to strengthen mutual understanding and co-operation. Among the goals of LINGUAPAX are:

- basing LINGUAPAX in the culture of peace, in UNESCO's endeavour to promote a spirit of tolerance, to defend the cause of human rights and develop education for democracy;
- defending minority and less favoured languages in relation to the promotion of foreign languages.

One brief classroom example of an exercise designed to achieve these goals is combating stereotypes through foreign-language teaching. Students are given foreign-language texts containing such stereotypes as *les Français sont séducteurs, les Allemands sont travailleurs, les Espagnols sont intrépides* and *les Anglais sont impassibles . . . !* After translating the texts, the students are asked to reflect upon stereotypes and how they impede understanding and communication. They discuss how stereotypes are developed and how they can be overcome.

FOUNDATIONS FOR TOLERANCE AND NON-VIOLENCE

The Pop Against Racism Foundation was founded in 1993 in reaction to the mounting tide of xenophobia and rapid decline in tolerance among young people in the Netherlands. Its policy is to expand knowledge, collaboration, tolerance and mutual understanding among young people in the country, particularly in the 12 to 20 age range. Its main activities in 1994 were:

- 'Racism Beat It' pop festival;
- a 'Racism Beat It' educational kit for use in music classes in secondary schools;
- the 'Racism Beat It' tour, a thematic drive-in show for secondary schools, part of a special week of tolerance among people from different cultural backgrounds;
- the 'Racism Beat It' karaoke show at the National Cultural Youth Event;
- an art project in co-operation with the World Jamboree Foundation.

The educational foundation to prevent violence in Argentina (FUNPREVI) is a non-profit institution created in 1990 to study the causes and effects of violence in Argentine society. The prevention of violence in all its forms is its main objective and its principal action is the implementation of education programmes. The foundation works to inform the public about victims' rights and advises on anti-violence legislation, provides education about violence to professionals and volunteers, and maintains Telefono de los Niños, a telephone assistance service offered to child victims of violence. It also organizes seminars for students, teachers and other professionals to promote adherence to non-violence.

HEALING WOUNDS TO IDENTITY

National and ethnic conflict can inflict deep wounds on identity. Healing such wounds is part of the mission of the Osnova School which has been working with the Primary School for Refugee Children from Bosnia and Herzegovina since 1992. The Osnova School also emphasizes the value of solidarity in its support of the educational need of refugee children to continue to be educated in their own cultural framework.

The Refugee School is taking part in a mutual peace education project with the Osnova School, the main purpose of which is to strengthen and preserve the refugee children's national consciousness, a necessary basis for the reconstruction of their destroyed homeland.

THEATRE TO INTERPRET CULTURE AND MEANING

In October 1993, Zarina Khan, a writer, producer and specialist in children's rights, went to Sarajevo. Her experience in working with young students in difficult situations, helping them to find their own means of expression, led her to this besieged city where schooling itself was directly endangered by the war.

Khan met thirteen young people from six different secondary schools in Sarajevo. Together, they decided to write *The Dictionary of Life*, a stage play about an alien from outer space on a mission to Earth to compile a dictionary of humankind, who lands in Sarajevo. The student-playwrights used this story to express their own personal vision of humanity, while exposing humankind's glaring contradictions.

In war-torn Sarajevo, over 1,000 spectators gathered to enjoy the creative energy of the young people. When it was over, 16-year-old Dina said, 'When I'm able to give my emotions to others, I feel like a winner. Theatre is our victory.'

The play is now available in Arabic, English, French, German, Greek, Polish, Romany, Russian, Slovak and Solvene.[1] It has been staged in seventy towns in France and in several other countries.

'Hourrah pour la Vie!' is a theatrical project of the Collège de l'Étoile in Port-au-Prince, Haiti, and the CO Voirets School in Geneva. The Lycée Houffon in Benin also participated in the project under the title 'Rencontre de l'Amitié.' The Haitian and the Swiss schools organized a multi-cultural theatre play with the aim of learning to work and live together. Each group rehearsed separately before joint rehearsals. By using video- and audio-cassettes, each group could follow the other group's work before they met for the first time for common rehearsals. The objective of the play, written and rehearsed by drama-teachers from the schools, was to combine different cultures in text, dance, movement and songs.

Solidarity, a value to be developed out of tolerance and empathy, was the basis of a theatre project for the secondary students at the Lycée

---

1. Copies can be obtained from Cie Zarina Khan, 6, rue des Petites Écuries, 75010 Paris, France.

Motema-Mpiko in Zaire. This project encouraged the development of the creative capacities of students by having them write plays about some of the problems of intolerance evident in their own lives: family stress, egoism, school problems and street children.

Theatre to promote peace and solidarity was also used in Portugal. The International Year of the Family gave a school from Porta, Externato de Nossa Senhora de Paz, an occasion to work on some solidarity projects. The theme, 'Against violence, solitude and indifference – the Earth, a universal family', was considered throughout the school year in history classes and other subjects. Activities were designed to teach the students to look at the world and its history from a global perspective and to develop attitudes of co-operation and solidarity.

NETWORKING FOR PEACE EDUCATION

Networking and exchanges between schools are becoming a significant means to a number of the goals of education for tolerance, respect and responsibility.

The Fjell School in Norway is participating in a twinning programme with schools in Croatia and Slovenia. Exchange visits have been an important factor in their co-operation. The school also participates in the Project on Ecological and Co-operative Education (PEACE), started in 1988 as a project dedicated to children, young people and adults working together to solve problems of development and ecology within the framework of education for peace. PEACE involves schools and teachers' colleges in Canada, the Netherlands, Norway, the Russian Federation, Ukraine and the United States.

Using technology to provide children with experiences in cross-cultural consideration of common global problems was the purpose of the International Children's Computer Camp at the Ecological Session in July 1994. Organized by the Programme Systems Institute of the Russian Academy of Sciences and Pereslavl National Park, the camp offered a course in environmental education to 650 participants aged 7 to 16 from schools in the Russian Federation, Ukraine and Germany.

Among various ecological projects and games on the camp's agenda was the 'Rainbow Bridge in Summer', linking schools in the Russian Federation and Japan through computer networks to promote ecological education and language education. Students from Shimizu Junior/High Christian School and the Simonoseki Choufu Junior/High School participated in the project from the Japanese side. They used APICNET, a Japanese educational network that unites hundreds of Japanese secondary and higher schools, research institutes and business companies. Students at the camp took part from the Russian Federation side. Participants exchanged legends of their respective motherlands with illustrations.

A week-long project was conducted by the Grundeschule am Windmuhlenberg in Berlin (Germany) to establish communication between two classes, one from the eastern part of the city and one from the west. Pupils were asked, through portraits and video, to express and discuss their perceptions about each other. Throughout the week, both classes contributed to the production of a commemorative newspaper which helped to establish friendships and working contact between the two groups.

ASP CLASSROOM-BASED ACTIVITIES

There are many general activities currently practised in the UNESCO Associated Schools that help develop tolerance and international understanding. The following activities focusing on human rights/tolerance-based issues, understanding other cultures, and eliminating stereotypes of and prejudices against things unknown are reported by schools in Germany, Norway, Poland and the Russian Federation.

LECTURES FOLLOWED BY CLASS DISCUSSION

- On the various international conventions to protect human rights, the rights of the child, the rights of women, the rights of refugees, the rights of workers, etc., and specific articles within these conventions.
- On the various regional conventions, the human-rights history of countries in these regions, with examples of tolerant and intolerant behaviour to demonstrate when these conventions have been respected or abused. Materials used included: video documentaries, newspaper and magazine reports, photographs, maps, etc. Questions discussed: How could those situations where intolerant behaviour manifested itself have been more peacefully resolved? What are the legal procedures for conflict resolution in regard to human rights?
- Small group discussions, followed by class discussions, on the meaning of poems, music, novels, etc., on the themes of tolerance, solidarity and human rights; on the meaning of words such as tolerance, democracy, government and peace, and their opposites; and on various types of intolerance.

GROUP RESEARCH ASSIGNMENTS

- Studying the history and origins of the United Nations; its role in protecting the rights of countries and peoples; its specific functions with relation to the Security Council, peacekeeping and peacemaking; its specialized agencies, and their functions and activities; studying of other national and international organizations which seek to protect human rights.

- Compiling of biographies on pacifist historical figures, philosophers, writers, cultural and religious groups who fought against injustice, torture or oppression, e.g. Gandhi, Martin Luther King.

STUDY OF DIFFERENT CULTURES

- Looking at cultures, both within the country and in their native countries – their customs, traditions, religion, written and oral forms of communication, festivals and food; field trips to cultural sites, to churches of different denominations, to cultural centres, to war museums, to exhibitions which have relevance to class topics and to battlefields. Encouraging the students to write to people in these countries. Some activities pursued to explore personal attitudes and values with relation to human rights/tolerance-based issues and to demonstrate how these affect the students' interactions with other students, family and community, were reported by the Council for Education in World Citizenship in the United Kingdom.
- Answering questionnaires on 'How tolerant are you?' with class surveys examining a range of responses to given situations in the school, home and community. These are afterwards discussed in class.
- Writing essays or poems, drawing charts and illustrations on the meaning of peace, tolerance, conflict resolution, etc.

The French Federation of UNESCO Clubs described activities to increase students' self-awareness and assertiveness when confronted with situations where tolerance or prejudice is an issue, for instance role plays followed by discussion on different types of behaviour and how and why these should be changed.

Another category of activities designed to promote positive attitudes and to encourage the practice of supportive, tolerant and compassionate behaviour in everyday life included:

- school exhibitions and plays;
- collections for the poor;
- visits to old people's homes, hospitals and community centres;
- organizing exchanges between schools in different socio-economic areas or with different cultures.

Both within and outside the school, a wide range of projects and activities are and can be undertaken to provide students with significant experiences in learning about human differences and common characteristics, and how these can constitute a source of personal enrichment and community strength.

Ten ideas for observing the International Day for Tolerance (16 November)

An International Day for Tolerance can serve as an annual occasion for debating the role of education in building tolerance as well as for wider social and political reflection and debate on local and global problems of intolerance, and as a moment to take stock of the progress made during the year and to propose fresh policies to close remaining gaps.

While the problem of intolerance is global, in the sense that it is on the increase in many parts of the world, the manifestations of intolerance usually take on local or national forms. Thus, in order to be effective, global norms against intolerance need to be combined with local, national and, not least, individual measures.

The ten ideas below are a starting point for thinking about how the observance of an International Day for Tolerance could help to boost the promotion of tolerance in individual countries and in the world. These proposals seek to involve mainly, but not exclusively, students and teachers from all countries in our collective quest for an intolerance-free world.

1. DIVERSITY IN YOUR COMMUNITY

Wherever you live, the wide diversity of your community will probably surprise you. It has been said that a culture is the sum total of all the influences that a region has undergone. Undertake an investigative project on cultural diversity in your town or community. Who lives there? How do they live? Articles, interviews, posters or displays can be designed to highlight the range of identities and cultures. How is this demonstrated in music? Reflect on the number of traditions of music and dance you've come across, and the mutual influences they show. Organize a concert or cultural festivals that bring together a range of cultural traditions.

2. HUMAN RIGHTS

How are the rights of persons belonging to national, ethnic, religious, linguistic or other minorities guaranteed in your community, nation, region? How about indigenous people, migrant workers, asylum-seekers and refugees, disabled people? Are their rights promoted and protected? Do you find that your law-enforcement officials are adequately educated about human rights? Can you suggest ways to improve their attitudes or behaviour towards minorities?

3. Do-it-yourself tolerance programme

Write your own tolerance curriculum or programme. This means deciding what are the component parts of tolerance, and how you think tolerant values can best be transmitted. Scrutinize your textbooks and televisions, newspapers and magazines for stereotyping, including gender typing, and assumptions about nationalities and ethnic groups. What are the tolerance priorities for your country or region?

4. No to violence

How does violence come into a community, school or home, and how can it be stopped? Act out the dynamics of tolerance and intolerance through role-playing, dialogue, dilemma-solving. Organize public debates, take sides in a debate, and then switch sides and speak for the opposite position. How do you imagine peaceful co-existence of diverse individuals and groups? What makes it work, and what undermines it?

5. Ecological diversity and human diversity

Every community is based on interdependence. Like the plants and animals, we couldn't survive if we were all the same. What are concrete examples of how a culture of peace and tolerance can promote environmental preservation? Start a project in your school or neighbourhood.

6. Religious tolerance

Organize events with the participation of different religious and non-religious groups in your community to discuss how tolerance is taught by these communities. How is tolerance taught by the different religions of the world, including the traditions of indigenous peoples? Each of them, in their own way, is founded on love and justice, and cannot be used to justify violence or war. Dialogue and discussion between representatives of many religious groups is a tradition that goes back centuries, and is still valuable today.

7. Current events

Organize discussions about current events in relation to tolerance and intolerance. Analyse actual conflicts of the past and present. How might they have been resolved or avoided? How is the issue of human rights in the news today? What are the fundamental rights and freedoms recognized by the international community? How do multicultural, multilinguistic countries work? What are the common interests that diverse peoples share?

8. SPORTS AND TOLERANCE

What are the international sporting events and what is their purpose? What are the possible links between sports and intolerance (such as exclusion of those unable to compete, competitive chauvinism and violence) and how may these be remedied? Organize an athletic event around the theme of diversity and tolerance.

9. CREATIVITY AT WORK

Art speaks volumes. Examine the work of an artist from another region of the world; what does it communicate to you? Create short stories, plays, poems, songs, articles, paintings, posters, photographs, or videos elucidating the themes of tolerance, and publish or distribute them. Write letters to prominent people, asking questions and communicating your views on the subject of tolerance.

10. INTERNATIONAL LINK-UPS

Start an international conversation or school-pairing project, by mail or computer. Write to others in another country about issues and problems you face in your lives. Exchange audio cassettes or pictures. Explore the possibilities of participating in international summer camps or student exchanges. Ask your school to join UNESCO's Associated Schools Project.

FOR STUDY AND DISCUSSION: PLANNING OUR OWN EFFORTS

Although limited in scope, this resource guide provides a basis to enable schools to take some steps towards education for tolerance. Begin your own school's efforts with a consideration of these questions:

▶ What goals and objectives should be set for our efforts to educate for tolerance?

▶ What elements and examples can we adapt from this resource?

▶ What additional resources do we need?

▶ What resources do we already have in our community or school?

▶ What materials and approaches can be developed to contribute to our own and UNESCO's efforts to promote education for tolerance?

▶ How will we assess the achievements of our programme?

6. Popular education and popular movements: learning for democracy and peace

Popular education: an impetus towards a culture of peace

A major basis of the current trend towards democracy is comprised of various popular movements throughout the world. Through these movements, citizens are taking responsibility for the well-being of their own communities. Some of these projects are educating to restore tolerance and respect to countries and communities torn by strife, bitter conflict and civil war. A number of the approaches and techniques are readily transferable to other areas and to formal education, especially teacher preparation.

Because the methods of popular education are designed for adults, it is appropriate to offer a few more detailed examples in this unit addressed to adult learners in both formal and non-formal settings.

Many communities have confronted their problems and produced solutions through popular education movements. Such movements view the problems that confront particular communities and the global society as problems of learning. Learning is conceptualized as a participatory process taking place at both the social and individual levels. Individuals develop knowledge and skills which contribute to the capacity of communities to deal with their problems. Individuals taking up their communal responsibilities enter into programmes of co-operative learning through which they analyse and confront their common problems.

Training of trainers in a participatory methodology

Popular education in its recent successes in the areas of community development, conflict resolution and human rights has demonstrated the efficacy of using the experiences of the participants in the learning process. In such processes, the role of the trainer is as crucial as the role of the teacher in the classroom. Indeed, many of the same educational principles apply to both, and some of the same methods, as noted, can be adapted to the classroom as well as the popular learning setting. The instructions for the trainers in a session for 'Training of Trainers on Women's Rights as Human Rights,' conducted in 1993 in Cambodia under the auspices of a non-governmental organization very active in this field, the People's Decade for Human Rights Education, comprise one such methodology. A few extracts can serve to provide the main features of this kind of training.[1]

WOMEN'S RIGHTS AS HUMAN RIGHTS

Objectives. This course has two main objectives: to teach human rights from a woman's perspective and to do so using participatory methodology. The unique aspect of the training is that it draws on women's life experiences to understand human-rights documents.

Principles of participatory methodology. The main principles of this methodology are the following:

- The life experience of the trainees is considered valuable and an essential input into the training. Unlike traditional methods of education, the trainer also learns during the process. There is an exchange of information, with both the trainee and trainer contributing valuable knowledge to each other.
- Crucial to the success of the training is that the participants and trainers have an opportunity to get to know each other. The entire first day is dedicated to this process, and throughout the workshop, activities are centred around building a lasting solidarity among the women.
- The participants learn by doing. The lecture method is kept to a minimum and the activities are structured so that all participants are involved. Small group discussions ensure that everyone's voice is heard.
- Great emphasis is placed on the feedback trainees give to the trainers. Trainees are asked daily what they would add or like to change about the

---

1. The full set of instructions for a three-day training course is available from the People's Decade for Human Rights Education, 526 West 111th Street, New York, NY 10025, USA; this organization can provide training manuals from various parts of the world.

activities. If they feel something is not useful, it is eliminated from the manual. Positive feedback is equally important to let the trainers know what exercises are effective.

The role of the trainer. A unique aspect of this training is the role played by the trainer. Unlike traditional training, the trainer is not just the knower, but the learner as well. She encourages the participants to contribute to the learning process by voicing their experiences. Because a large part of the training is centred around the life experiences of the trainees, it is important that the trainer adequately acknowledge their input and show compassion towards them. It is important to be open about her own life experiences as well, especially if they are similar to those of the participants. She is receptive to points of view that differ from her own and is willing to make changes in the structure of the course if need be. In general, she must be flexible. If something is not working in the day's activities, she needs to be able to make quick, practical decisions as to how to improve the exercises.

To illustrate the processes that could be used in other adult education programmes, two activities are reproduced from the training manual.

Activity: Identifying and reflecting on women's roles in Khmer society.

Objectives: To increase awareness of the societal expectations placed on women.

Procedure: Break the trainees up into small groups and ask them to come up with three roles that women play in Khmer society (for example, wife, mother, daughter). Ask them to list the expectations society has for them in those roles. Next, ask them to discuss how they feel about these expectations. Are they fair or unfair? Each group elects a spokesperson to report back to the large group.

(The following activity is carried out simultaneously in separate rooms: women in one room, men in another.)

Activity: Identify women's rights that should be legislated for the protection of dignity.

Objective: To think about what rights women want protected by legislation.

Procedure: First, ask each trainee to compose a list of rights she/he would like protected. Second, break up into small groups (women in one group, men in another) and ask each group to come up with a list of ten rights. Each group elects a spokesperson to report back. The trainer should ask each group for one right at a time while writing them on the board.

Activity: Comparison of the trainees' list with human-rights documents.

Objective: To illustrate the similarities between the trainees list and the United Nations documents (such as the Convention on the Elimination of All Forms of Discrimination Against Women, or the Universal Declaration of Human Rights) and to point out the limitations of the official documents.

Procedure: The trainer points out similarities between the trainees' list and various articles of the Convention and the Declaration, thereby validating the trainees' efforts. The trainer also highlights particular articles in which the trainees had been more detailed than the official documents, particularly as they relate to their daily reality.

Activity: Having the men come up with two lists of rights, one for themselves and one for a significant woman in their lives.

Objectives: To have the men think about women's rights as human rights.

Procedure: The trainees as trainers ask the men to list the rights they would like to see protected by legislation (fifteen minutes), then ask them to break up into small groups and have each group come up with a list of ten rights (twenty minutes). Ask them to come up with another list of rights they would like to see legislated for a significant woman in their lives (wife, mother, daughter) for another twenty minutes. A spokesperson is elected from each group and the trainees as trainers write each of their lists on the board.

Activity: Comparing the two men's lists with the women's list.

Objective: To compare, contrast and discuss all the lists.

Procedure: Bring all the groups back together and ask the trainees as trainers in charge to post the women's list and the two men's lists side by side. Start with looking at the list of rights the men came up with for the women. Point out common points with the women's list. When the men's list of women's rights is exhausted, the women read the additional rights from their list, discussing each one and encouraging the men to accept them.

Activity: Developing strategies to defend, promote and protect women's rights.

Objective: To share strategies on how to promote women's rights as a community concern.

Procedure: Ask the women to express to the men how they would want to be supported on women's rights. Ask the men to suggest some effective strategies to support some of the human rights mentioned in the women's list and in their list for women.

Activity: Rehearsing theatre presentations on articles of the Convention for the afternoon.

Objectives: To use participatory theatre to train men in women's rights.

Procedure: Explain participatory theatre. Have the two groups prepare and rehearse their presentations according to the selected articles in the Convention. Remind them that each member of the group must take part and that they have approximately twenty minutes for each presentation.

People's Decade for Human Rights Education.

FOR STUDY AND DISCUSSION: WOMEN'S RIGHTS

▶ Would the themes and format of the foregoing training session be suitable in your community? If not, what form of training on the issues of human rights and/or women's rights would be appropriate?

▶ What do you believe to be the relationship between human rights, including the equality of women, and a culture of peace?

Studying armed conflict and the escalation of the cycle of intolerance and violence

The great concern with intolerance articulated in the United Nations Declaration and the efforts undertaken during the United Nations Year for Tolerance derive primarily from the many armed conflicts to which various forms of intolerance have led. To move towards the resolution of these conflicts and towards eliminating the scourge of armed violence within and between nations, citizens need to reflect upon the causes of these conflicts and the various alternatives that may be available for their resolution. The Philippine Office of the Presidential Adviser on the Peace Process has published a study kit for citizens' groups seeking to educate themselves in order to contribute to the process. In a clear and simple format, with drawings illustrating questions and answers about the armed struggles in the Philippines, the basic causes of their own and of many similar conflicts in the world are presented. Excerpts could be adapted to the study of the causes of armed conflicts in many locations.

Five major causes were determined:

- massive poverty and economic inequity;
- poor governance;

- injustice and abuse of power;
- control of political power by a few;
- exploitation of cultural communities and lack of recognition of their ancestral domain.

Other causes:

- differences in political beliefs and ideology;
- foreign intervention and domination;
- moral decadence.

People also are concerned about:

- the destruction of the environment;
- continuing armed confrontation;
- the debilitating effects of armed conflicts on civilians in the battle zones. The booklet begins by describing the consequences and costs of the violence. This introduction, combined with information about the economic and social consequences of arms production and armed conflict, can in itself provide a good introductory unit on war and armed conflict for popular education and teacher-training programmes. It begins with a crucial question.

Quite simply we ask: are we going to continue fighting each other?

We have suffered enough from the continuing armed and violent confrontations in many parts of our country.

From 1973 to 1992, the death toll reached 55,471 – soldiers, government officials, rebels and innocent civilians. About 33,709 have been wounded and 1,832 are missing.

Some 1.5 million people have experienced displacement in the course of more than two decades of armed conflict. They were ordinary peasants, tribal and marginal Filipinos who were thus deprived of their sources of livelihood as well; and children who died of diseases, were orphaned and deprived of education because of the fighting.

Damage to crops and properties since 1982 has already been estimated at 1.38 billion pesos.

Furthermore, the government has had to spend billions in operations to maintain peace and order throughout the country under an environment of armed internal conflicts.

Perhaps if only half of this could have been spent on development and livelihood programmes, our country might be in a much better state today.

We could have already paid our debts.

We could have built more schools and health centres.

We could have had more funds for land reform and mass housing. Our government employees and workers could have had more decent pay. We could have set up more power generators and would not have had to endure long brownouts, and could have built infrastructure to prevent the pestering floods.

A rifle bullet costs five pesos. The cost of twenty-five bullets could thus be enough for a day's budget for an average family.

As the armed confrontations rage on, attaining progress becomes an ever more difficult task. Our country will be doomed to poverty, and will forever be at the tail-end of our fast-developing Asian neighbours.

The contending parties claim they are fighting for the sake of our country and our people. Yet it is our country and people as a whole who eventually suffer the most as the conflict goes on.

For so long a time have we longed and aspired for peace.

But even if there are many difficult obstacles, our dream of a genuine, just and lasting peace is not unattainable. If we are united, nothing is impossible. The peace that we all desire is within reach.

Our people's involvement is the key to the attainment of a genuine, just and lasting peace. Those involved in the conflict agree that the peace process cannot prosper unless it is anchored on the involvement and participation of all sectors of society.

A peace process should be community-based, reflecting the sentiments, values and principles important to all Filipinos. It shall not be defined by government alone, nor by the contending armed groups, but by all Filipinos as one community.

It is the goal of the peace process to establish a just, equitable, humane and pluralistic society.

It is aimed at peacefully resolving and ending the armed conflict, with neither blame nor surrender, but with dignity for all concerned.

Come then and let us march on the road to peace. Let us start now. Let us all participate. Let us enlighten ourselves on the issues, and realize how we can contribute towards the attainment of peace.

Philippine Peace Process, a kit prepared by the Office of the Presidential Adviser on the Peace Process, Manilla, Philippines, 1994.

Study based on such material should be followed, as it is in the booklet, with consideration of who comprises the various parties to the conflict, the goals they are pursuing, how each party perceives the others involved in the conflict, possibilities for the identification of common interests, what each party might be willing to accept as the basis for cessation of the armed struggle and various alternatives for a long-range solution which could produce a mutually advantageous, co-operative relationship between the conflicting parties.

The kit also contains material on the basic values and principles deemed necessary to guiding a process towards a just, comprehensive and lasting peace, materials on the longer and deeper post-conflict processes of reconciliation, rehabilitation and reconstruction, and an outline of a comprehensive process of six paths to peace. Thus it provides an overview of peace-making as a complex, holistic process of the kind fundamental to the conceptual framework on which this educational resource is based. It is a vehicle for demonstrating how tolerance opens the way to the longer and deeper processes of building a culture of peace.

Proposed continuing-training course in peace education

Some popular educators are proposing substantive courses in peace education. The following was produced in Nicaragua by the Centre for International Studies.

This training proposal seeks to develop a specialist field in conflict studies for the network of peace promoters, channelling knowledge and effort into improving organization, community development, economic management and legal consultancy within a framework contributing to and partaking in the strategic aim of peace with economic justice.

Justification

Taking into account the mechanisms decided on for training in this new phase, we have concluded that the latter should have a differentiated focus until the problem of uneven academic standards and powers of assimilation among promoters can be alleviated.

The objective would in any case be to provide the promoters with some technical support enabling them to develop those skills and aptitudes in social promotion and organization brought to light in the course of the work done, for the sake of better theme preparation at the local level.

The objective will ultimately be a qualitative improvement in the levels of specialization of the promoters, better quality in the work of reproducing workshops and greater evenness and consistency in the training process generally.

In this respect the training for promoters making up both the co-ordination and liaison team and the 'multipliers' will provide for a diversified and systematic research practice or process conducive to an accelerated learning process that can be transmitted to demobilized persons in other countries.

1. To provide a formal, systematic and specialized training course for two groups of forty peace and development promoters who would engage in organized educational activities with a multiplier effect, mediation, organization and community action.
2. To strengthen reconciliation through local use of the skills of war veterans and local leaders in conflict resolution.
3. To institutionalize community participation in the search for solutions to local conflicts, establishing the local popular mediation centres with the support of community leaders.

Basic training in conflict transformation (according to availability of fellowships), comprising:

- Spanish
- Computing
- Administration
- Accounting
- Languages
- Research methods
- General culture

Areas

1. Teaching methods (20 per cent)

- Principles and techniques of transformational education
- Dynamics of educational assimilation and integration
- Methods of planning and general educational assessment in addition to community mediation
- Procedures for the preparation and use of general teaching material and conflict transformation
- Techniques of educational assessment and group dynamics

2. Addressing conflicts (20 per cent)

- Conflict and peace: concepts
- Mediation techniques (II)
- Theory and practice of reconciliation
- Organizational and social conflicts
- Active non-violence

3. Law and justice (20 per cent)

- Rights
- Legislation and property
- Constitutional law
- Principles of penal law

- The judiciary in Nicaragua

4. Community development (15 per cent)
- Theory and methods of social organization
- Principles and methods of organization
- Legislation on and autonomy of municipalities
- Municipal development plan with citizen participation
- Principles and techniques of social communication

5. Globalization (10 per cent)
- World power
- The international economy
- International bodies, NGOs
- New concepts of security and the role of armies
- Global ecology
- Role of external co-operation and NGOs in Nicaragua

6. Options (10 per cent)
- Personal development (theory and practice)
- Local experience of economic rehabilitation
- Gender, development and peace
- Ecology
- Electoral training in collaboration with the Supreme Electoral Council

7. Comprehensive analysis (5 per cent)

Support for a National Peace Building Network and Training Program in Nicaragua, Centro de Estudios Internacionales, Apartado 1747, Managua, Nicaragua, 1995.

FOR STUDY AND DISCUSSION: POST-CONFLICT PEACE EDUCATION PROJECTS

▶ What similarities do you see between the Philippine Peace Process and the Proposal of the Nicaraguan Centro de Estudios Internacionales?

▶ What do you see as some of the fundamental principles for ending and transcending armed conflicts?

Peace-building: conflict transformation and reconciliation

The process of moving from intolerance through tolerance to peace, as has been argued here, can only be executed within the context of values and skills. When parties to a conflict understand that their ends will not be met through continued strife and that the well-being of all concerned would be improved by positive and co-operative relationships, they will place a high value on peace. The value, however, cannot be realized without the appropriate skills of conflict resolution, reconciliation and peace-building. Recognizing these realities and preparing to meet them is thus essential to reaching a culture of peace.

These imperatives are being implemented in a number of post-conflict situations, notable among them the work of the Managua Centre, now working to develop a national pool of community leaders capable of preventing and dealing with conflict, and of initiating and facilitating peace-building. Specifically, the programme seeks firstly:

> . . . to create incentives and to teach ex-soldiers and divided communities, the skills needed to contain violence at the base level, and secondly, to encourage the development of a local, sustainable capacity to manage problems and enhance democratic tolerance.
>
> The initiative pursues a comprehensive strategy to contain violence and polarization, particularly in northern Nicaragua, focusing on the creation of a national network of peace activists, drawn primarily from ex-combatants' organizations from both sides (Sandinista and Resistencia). These peace activists are trained in conflict resolution and community development. They operate at the local level and are capable of reproducing their skills and influence, thereby creating a national pool of community leaders capable of preventing and dealing with conflict.
>
> Over the past two years, these ex-combatants have formed their own organization, the Peace and Development Network. Based on international peace-building experiences and conflict resolution theory, they have prepared a programme of civic activities to be carried out in communities in conflict zones for use in northern Nicaragua where conflict is still serious.
>
> They employ a methodology and programme design based on interaction and integration skills, with reconciliation as a guiding principle and source of inspiration, and consensus-building for transformation as an objective. Through participation in case analysis and focused interactive exercises (simulations, role-playing and reproduction of tested scenarios), participants practise analysis and problem-handling skills and gain applied knowledge of different concepts.

Conflict transformation

The objective of this component is to make communities aware that their ability to identify the conflicts that caused the war will facilitate the identification of the methods needed to end the war. The programme concentrated on conflict identification, prevention and transformation, negotiation and third-party mediation, dispute resolution and public security issues. Each theme is geared to contribute to the transformation of a violent and military-oriented culture into one in which dialogue, tolerance and pluralism are prevalent.

This phase will deal with subjects such as concepts of conflict and conflict resolution, active non-violence, mediation and negotiation, psychological aspects of violence, stress management, non-violent communications, gender sensitivity, human-rights standards and contemporary international peace-building.

The training will include input on participation, human rights, social change, peace, development and democracy, techniques for community development, communication skills, group dynamics and the sociology of rural communities. This includes management skills, such as crisis administration, team-building, and managing diversity and organizational conflict. It aims at deploying the (National Peace Building) Network as a pool of trained personnel with a basic knowledge of the electoral system and its operational and legal procedures, capable of serving as civic monitors and enforcers of codes of conduct.

Each year, the programme will organize an international meeting for the groups involved in community peace-building and in the reintegration of demobilized soldiers. Participants will be peace promoters from Colombia, El Salvador, Guatemala, Mozambique, the Philippines and South Africa, countries where similar experiences have taken place.

The Education and Action for Peace Programme of the Centre involves:
1. Former soldiers of the armed forces and of the Nicaraguan resistance
2. Disabled veterans' organizations
3. Repatriates and displaced persons
4. Demobilized women's groups

Support for a National Peace Building Network and Training Program in Nicaragua, op. cit.

Reconciliation

In the process of moving from hostility and conflict towards tolerance and peace, reconciliation may be the most crucial stage. Some trainers and practitioners of conflict resolution – Nicaraguan trainer Zoilamerica Ortega for instance – assert that without reconciliation, conflict resolution is not possible. She points out that justice is just as essential to reconciliation, as reconciliation is to peace, and emphasizes the importance of conflict resolution.

Reconciliation, properly conceived as the construction of peace, far from ignoring, instead squarely faces the very unjust structures which give rise in the first place to social conflict. This is the type of reconciliation – a truly transformative reconciliation – that has in fact been advanced by many contemporary social movements.

In this context, reconciliation is conceived of as one component in the larger process of positive preservation or reconstruction of social identity. It is on the basis of the positive and liberating reaffirmation of social identity that the groundwork is laid for unity among the oppressed and the victims of violence, and for the conditions to emerge which allow those formerly in conflict to challenge those who oppress and who perpetuate violence.

Put another way, reconciliation becomes an expression of faith in a unity of purpose. Reconceiving reconciliation as a social rather than an individual process implies that reconciliation cannot be separated from structural change which allows the oppressed to recover their integrity. Logically, this type of reconciliation implies that conflict itself is not necessarily overcome, but it also allows us to put forward reconciliation as a liberating process which challenges the very basis of conflict and therefore opens the possibility of achieving an authentic peace based on justice.

The conception advanced here has allowed us to identify the underlying relation between reconciliation and conflict resolution as regards the demobilized in Nicaragua. It has facilitated *rapprochement* between population sectors divided by military conflict, in which the whole notion of reconciliation is one based on the resolution of a conflict within a social sector and the organic *rapprochement* between members of this sector, rather than an agreement reached between political leaders.

Reconciliation, therefore, is less the restoration of formal political stability than a means for restoring shared identity and organic unity among members of a social group, in this case the popular sectors in Nicaragua, and for promoting democratic transformation.

From the viewpoint of formal conflict-resolution techniques, reconciliation tends to be seen as a necessary first step, or precondition, which paves the way for formal negotiations between political leaders. Reconciliation is therefore viewed as a means for establishing negotiating procedures. But when it is concerned with the reunification of groups within the same social class, reconciliation must be viewed as a process designed to build mutual trust and respect as the first phase in a broader exchange leading to conscious and positive social action. Techniques of reconciliation must therefore move beyond the notion of merely removing the obstacles to direct negotiation.

> To summarize, we conceive of reconciliation as a process which promotes organic unity among those who had formerly been at war with one another by addressing those conditions which gave rise in the first place to war. Such a conceptualization allows for the conscious involvement of former antagonists in negotiation and conflict resolution and lays the groundwork for peaceful coexistence on the basis of reconstructed or newly constructed shared identities and interests.
>
> Zoilamerica Ortega M., *Reconciliation between Former Sandinista Soldiers and Members of the Resistance*, Managua, Centro de Estudios Internacionales, October 1994. (Research Paper series.)

FOR STUDY AND DISCUSSION: PEACE-BUILDING

▶ What are the most critical areas for peace-building based on tolerance?

▶ To what other areas of the world might a similar process of peace-building be applied?

▶ How do the components of the programme conducted by the Centro de Estudios Internacionales relate to the content, methods and goals of education for tolerance set forth in this resource?

▶ What seem to be the basic principles of reconciliation? Are these principles applicable to other types of conflicts?

▶ Can you suggest some specific reconciliation actions or steps to be taken in the suggested situation? In the resolution of other conflicts about which you are concerned?

Workers' education: 'Facing Hatred'

Labour organizations play a very important role in adult education and address many issues of social concern, including tolerance. One example of that role was a seminar on 'Facing Hatred', an initiative that could be replicated in many countries and communities. The seminar deemed networking and co-operative efforts to be extremely important in the struggle for tolerance.

Over fifty labour educators from four continents participated in the 'Facing Hatred' seminar (Israel, October 1993) sponsored by the International Federation of Workers' Education Associations (IFWEA). Among many topics discussed in relation to hatred were 'political and educational experiments in grappling with hatred in Germany, the building of bridges between the races in South Africa, the civil war in former

Yugoslavia, reducing prejudice using the education system, the role of the media and non-governmental organizations, nation-building versus religion in India, the Jewish-Arab conflict and the struggle against anti-semitism.

The seminar drew some significant conclusions and adopted the following guidelines:

> Hatred is an acquired attitude and therefore not a built-in element of human nature.
>
> Education can and should play a fundamental role for the purpose of achieving social justice. Education policy-makers are therefore called upon to be receptive to all innovations inside and outside educational institutions in facing hatred with the aim of including the issue in general curricula.
>
> Education about values for democracy and social justice should be included at all stages of education, including the education of educators, and increased co-operation with teachers and their organizations should be developed. The interest shown by Education International (a confederation of teachers' unions) in this context was honoured by the seminar.
>
> A closer network of communication between the member organizations of IFWEA should be developed as well as a database with the aim of exchanging information and experiences.
>
> IFWEA is urged to develop further regional and international co-operation schemes to deepen and broaden educational endeavours against all forms of political hatred. The seminar emphasized the need for special efforts in this context in the Middle East.
>
> IFWEA is urged to establish alliances with organizations working on the same projects in order to co-ordinate better and work more effectively. Co-operation, already started with Amnesty International ('Another Way' seminar in Oslo) and other non-governmental organizations, is considered extremely important for IFWEA.
>
> The 'Facing Hatred' seminar concluded by underlining the importance of contacts, co-operation, and support among relevant institutions and organizations in the work of facing hatred.
>
> *Workers' Education*, Bulletin of the International Federation of Workers' Education Associations (IFWEA), No. 3, December 1993.

Literacy education: poetry and social change

An African community development literacy programme, TOSTAN, has produced a number of learning modules useful to many adult non-formal educators. These modules encourage self-expression and participation.

While every module makes learners look critically at their surroundings, TOSTAN, a Senegalese non-governmental organization, has been successful in using social mobilization to reinforce the education classes. UNICEF and OXFAM-America have sponsored poetry-debate sessions in national languages in TOSTAN classes. Working with traditional musicians and singers, a Senegalese poet, Thierno Seydou Sall, visited education classes to recite poetry in Wolof, then lead discussions on issues that are often taboo.

Through these sessions, people have started to think about their feelings and their rights. As one woman who attended the poetry session said, 'We all had these ideas before but we dared not say anything. Now we have the courage to stand up and say what we really think.' TOSTAN frequently receives poems from women written after the workshop and they reflect a new-found confidence.

This poem was written by Soxna Ngiraan, a 34-year-old participant from Kër Sayib. It has been translated from Wolof.

The First Wife of a Not-So-Good Man

I am the first wife of a not-so-good man
And I am frustrated.
I married before others married
Struggled before others struggled
Tired before others tired
In order for my family to succeed.
I have known hunger
I have known thirst
In order for my family to succeed.
Yet how did you thank me, not-so-good man?
You waited until I was old
And had many children. . . .
Then you married a young girl
And placed her high above me.
Whatever you have, you give to her
Whatever you hear, you tell her
I no longer see you.
I no longer talk to you.
If I quarrel with her, you say it's my fault.
If we argue, you tell me to leave.
I no longer have a voice in this house
And my children are suffering too.
So will I ever experience the success

I so fervently sought?
The Wolof say:
'Where there has been a fire
It is difficult for a plant to grow.'

A community education project on children's rights

The Convention on the Rights of the Child is deemed by some to be the most comprehensive statement on human rights of all the international standards. Were these rights of the child to be fully implemented, children would grow in a state of peace and in a process of learning and development that produces peaceful individuals and societies. The rights of the child also provide excellent subject-matter for education for peace and tolerance in the present. Many learning experiences for all kinds of settings are based upon this topic, sometimes explicitly on the convention and sometimes simply on the concepts and values of the human rights of children. Because of its comprehensiveness, this topic lends itself to holism in methodology and to the community development objectives. Here is one such initiative from the same non-governmental organization in Senegal which brings together various generations in a community education project involving two villages who have come together to review and assess the project.

This is part of the non-formal basic education programme in national languages initiated in 1988 and implemented in Thiès by TOSTAN, in collaboration with UNICEF and CIDA.

[At a community gathering], children and adults sit on the floor, on mats or on small wooden seats. . . . Facing them is a big map, a blackboard, a flipchart and a table.

Several signs with written texts in Wolof are to be seen all over the village: on the trees, on the wooden fences, on the houses themselves. They are part of an effort to create a 'literate environment', surrounding both adults and children with written texts. Streets have been baptized with such names as 'Street of Knowledge' and 'Street of Peace'. The *boutique* (a small village shop where mainly matches, oil and salt are sold), which together with the school is the only 'modern' cement house in the village, displays on its façade a sign in Wolof that reads: 'Boutique – Choose What You Want'.

The literacy facilitator is the master of ceremonies. He has made the drawings to illustrate children's rights, prepared his students, and promoted and organized this encounter. Everything is conducted in Wolof, one of Senegal's six national languages.

A series of songs introduce the act. The alphabet song seems to be one of the most popular ones: the words remain the same, but each village puts it to its own melody, some of them with choruses. Most of the songs have been written by the students with the help of their facilitator. Thus, through music and rhythm, they welcome the visitors, praise the facilitator and acknowledge the organizations in charge of the education programme. A special song has been created on children's rights.

The facilitator announces the official start of the programme and explains it at length to the audience. Then he begins to unfold the flipchart.

Children of the world

The first picture is an introduction to the flipchart and presents children of different races from different countries, wearing different costumes. The facilitator asks the students to describe what they see in the picture, and then asks them to point out differences in the children. Children of all ages insistently raise their hands and snap their fingers. They all want to speak. They give all sorts of answers: the hair, the shoes, the skin colour, the height, the clothes, the eyes. He then asks what their similarities are and the children again answer: they are all people, they all have joys and problems, they all have to eat food. One small girl shyly states: 'All the children have rights.' Everyone claps. Now the facilitator asks for a volunteer to come to the front, identify and choose a sheet of paper on which a text is written corresponding to the subject of the drawing, in this case, 'All the children of the world have rights'. A girl comes to the front to perform this part of the presentation: she studies the different sheets displayed on the table, picks the right sheet and then 'reads' it aloud while turning around several times so that the phrase is visible to the entire audience. While 'read' is here a verb between inverted commas – these young learners have started school only two months ago – since it is rather a case of visually recognizing words and phrases, this is actually the very first step to real reading, to reading with meaning and with fun! . . .

The whole presentation on children's rights will follow this pattern: introduction of the picture; questions to children on what they see illustrated; discussion of the specific right suggested by the picture; interpretation of the right by the children through a short, often provocative, dramatization or poem they have created; discussion of the play or poem; and identification and reading aloud of small texts written on sheets of paper and which correspond to the drawings. Following are some examples of the rights presented.

The right to a clean environment

The picture shows a woman with a broom, cleaning up her yard, and several garbage baskets aligned by the fence of the house. After discussion, the children present a skit in which they have been working on a village clean-up and are discussing further actions to assure success. Then an older man comes along and throws down paper from the food he has been eating. When the children try to explain to him that he should not dirty the environment, since they are working to clean it up, he becomes angry and says that children do not have the right to tell adults what to do. Discussion follows this skit among the children and the adults. The facilitator asks, 'What will happen in the future if everyone continues to pollute the environment?' The children respond in unison. 'Our whole country will be a garbage pile!' The adults are delighted with this outburst. . . .

The right not to work too much

In this drawing, a girl is busy with many domestic chores. An 8-year-old girl comes to the front and reads a poem that speaks of a girl who does all the work in the house and has no time to play. She ends the poem with: 'At night, when I finally lie down to sleep, I think and think and think about my life. My heart is full and I begin to cry because I do not know when all this suffering will end.' Adults – and particularly mothers – seem uncomfortable and distressed.

A parenthesis on children's responsibilities

At this point, a sheet on responsibilities is inserted in the flipchart, apparently to counterbalance the many rights of children and the increasing anxiety of parents. There are no pictures on this paper, only written text. The facilitator asks the children to name their responsibilities and duties. Some of the answers are: to be polite, to be respectful, to love oneself, love one's country, to be obedient, to help out, to promote peace.

A father in the audience thanks the children because they have brought a lot of knowledge to the adults. A mother says that it is the first time that two neighbouring communities have met together. And this is thanks to the education of both the children and the adults. A young boy, full of enthusiasm, jumps into the centre of the stage and starts to dance. Someone grabs a huge plastic bowl and uses it as a drum.

And the big party begins. Girls and boys, children and adults are all in the mood to dance. . . .

We have witnessed a memorable occasion in the lives of these children and adults, and of these villages. Nothing here has been conventional. Education and rights, school and life, students and parents, parents and teachers, teachers and students, reading-writing and singing-dancing, flipchart, poems and plays: they all seemingly interact and go together naturally, as if in a continuum. And this is why conventional categories and classifications – such as formal/non-formal/informal education or school/out-of-school or the distinction between children/adolescents/adults or between children's education and adult education or even the term community participation – do not help to capture and explain what this is all about. . . .

Children and adults learning together, becoming literate and aware together, in a genuine family and community learning process.

Cynthia Guttmann, *Breaking Through: TOSTAN's Non-Formal Basic Education Programme in National Languages in Senegal,* New York/Paris, UNICEF/UNESCO, 1995. (Making it Work, Education for All Innovation Series, 6.)

FOR STUDY AND DISCUSSION: COMMUNITY EDUCATION FOR TOLERANCE

▶ What benefits would such a community education project bring to a community? Could all communities benefit from intergeneration education for tolerance?

▶ What issues of tolerance would be most appropriate for such an educational initiative in your community?

▶ What role can culture and the popular arts play in education for tolerance?

Conflict resolution: skills of tolerance and peace

Skills for dealing with conflict are essential goals of adult and popular education as they are of formal schooling for tolerance. A project in Lebanon attempts to build tolerance and peace after years of civil war through training in conflict skills which are described in a manual. A few extracts are given here.

Conflict exists in human life, even in peaceful times, and brings with it some constructive and beneficial processes in addition to the heavy costs, suffering and destructive forces. The purpose of conflict resolution is to remove or mitigate the negative results and destruction of conflict, while preserving its beneficial, life-giving qualities.

Conflict resolution combines in a problem-solving process the values contained in other concepts: from human rights, a deep respect for human dignity and for the legitimacy and capacity of every person; from democracy, the values of participation and responsiveness within a changing world environment; and from peace, the value of acceptance of the other and satisfaction in non-violent interaction. Conflict resolution is a process of decision-making whose objectives are to handle, manage, settle or resolve conflict in ways which enhance the values of the other three concepts.

Conflict resolution has a positive goal as the basic human needs of all parties are fulfilled by the new equilibrium. A few conflicts achieve full resolution in this sense; many more are settled or managed in ways which permit the parties to move on to other issues and problems with at least partial satisfaction of their interests and needs.

Experiences in trying to resolve conflict yield as many insights on what not to do in conflict situations as they do on what to do.

There are different levels of intensity in conflict, which can range from mild disagreements . . . to violent conflict.

The nature of the conflict may also vary depending on its subject matter. While each conflict has its unique qualities and differences in intensity and subject matter, it often shares many common characteristics. Emotional anger and frustration, fear, lack of communication, tendencies to blame and dehumanize the other, escalation, strategic choices for violence or negotiation and mediation – these factors and others can be found in . . . conflicts which sometimes explode into violence. Forms may change, but underlying qualities can be the same or very similar.

Parties often bring with them into today's conflict long histories of perceived grievances and animosity. These personal or group memories can be heavy luggage that must be unpacked, identified, evaluated and appreciated by all parties before issues are ready to be resolved. Such reconciliation at a deep level is challenging for most people, no matter what the problem, whether in a family, a community or internationally. . . .

Past sacrifices tie parties to a disastrous history in present conflicts but, if the future is to be different, those in conflict must assume this past in a way that does not deny its existence or importance, or allow it to be used as a recipe for an equally disastrous future. Apologies and forgiveness are often helpful in this reconciliation process, but they are rarely offered in serious conflict. All sides think they are victims suffering at the hands of the other, having been required by difficult circumstances to behave as they did. Yet, only when they each hear the other express an appreciation of the wrongs and sufferings caused, can they acknowledge the past together and forget it in order to embrace a better future.

Resolving conflict is made even more complex by the existence of institutional or structural obstacles, cultural differences and constantly changing conditions.[2]

People can learn important skills to help them manage, settle or resolve their conflicts more effectively: good listening and communication skills; understanding the psychology of inter-personal contact; working constructively with others; [avoiding] behaviour which maintains or intensifies conflict; identifying the destructive forces of anger, fear, blame or selective perception. . . .

Participation by all interested parties is basic to conflict resolution. The interested parties should include not only those whose support is necessary to the success of a good outcome, but also those whose opposition would pose a serious obstacle to its smooth implementation. Including actual and potential opponents, together with supporters, creates a more difficult process to manage constructively but it brings many benefits. Problems are defined jointly and become shared problems for all participants. Parties experience a sense of satisfaction in working together on seemingly intractable issues and they come out with a commitment to make the resulting solution work.

Conflict resolution recognizes that a wise and durable agreement must fulfil certain basic human needs for all parties: needs for security, identity, recognition, participation and development. Yet, someone caught in violent conflict tends to see the price of fulfilling his or her own needs as direct cost to the other parties in giving up their demands for the same needs. Especially in protracted and deep-rooted conflict, parties must create opportunities for appreciating that these basic human needs are not in limited supply, that each party can satisfy its own needs without asking others to compromise or concede theirs.

Judicial systems are an example of an institutional form of conflict resolution provided by society. The law existing in the local jurisdiction sets the standards by which disputes that go through the courts are decided. Most deep-rooted and protracted conflict, however, is not effectively handled in the courts because the values embedded in the existing legal system are usually central to the conflict. What is needed for these conflicts is a forum which helps re-establish consensus on values in the community. Typically, in serious conflict, a third party is needed to help design and manage such a process, facilitate an exploration of the values in conflict, and help the parties search for a solution acceptable to all.

---

2. The various symptoms and manifestations of intolerance outlined in Chapter 2 also add complexity to many conflicts. – Ed.

Third-party mediators are important intervening forces in conflict resolution. They do not pose a threat to the parties because they have no power to dictate a solution. However, they do bring the power of ideas, of information and of process skills. Mediators can help break down stereotypes which distort communication and perception; they can widen the vision and deepen the understanding of the conflict to generate opportunities for a creative solution; they can identify and explore goals which the parties could never raise themselves; they can give parties a face-saving excuse to escape from public entrapment in escalating conflict spirals; and, lastly, they can reframe issues so that parties see win/win solutions rather than either/or options.

The form of the conflict resolution process is limited only by the imagination and inventiveness of those who wish to use it. Many groups and organizations which experience regular disputes, grievances or conflict, design special procedures that permit full participation by those affected and establish accepted standards by which they can evaluate the fairness of a proposed solution. Often they encourage negotiation first, then provide some form of mediation and, finally, if resolution is still not reached, require a more formal arbitration of the outstanding issues.

Sanàa Osseiran, *Handbook: Resource and Teaching Material in Conflict Resolution, Education for Human Rights, Peace and Democracy*, pp. 1–3, Paris, International Peace Research Association (IPRA)/UNESCO, 1995.

FOR STUDY AND DISCUSSION: CONFLICT RESOLUTION

▶ What are the major skills of conflict resolution and who should learn them?
▶ How could the adults in your community be offered conflict skills training?
▶ Could you design an adult education programme for human rights, conflict resolution, reconciliation and peace-building for your community?
▶ What agencies and organizations might provide such training?

Appendices

1. Resources

Many communities and educators will want to do far more in educating for tolerance than is made possible by this limited resource. For those wishing to further develop or to enrich the educational efforts they have undertaken with this guide, the following sources are listed. It should be noted, however, that these are but a few of the many sources now in existence.

Organizations offering services and resources for educators

Anthropology Outreach and Public Information Office
Department of Anthropology
NHB 363 MRC 112,
Smithsonian Institution,
Washington, D. C. 20560
United States

Multiculture Educational Resource Collection,
Instructional Resources Branch,
Box 7, Main Floor,
1181 Portage Avenue,
Winnipeg, Manitoba R3G 0T3,
Canada

Anne Frank Stichting,
Postbus 730,
1000 AS Amsterdam,
The Netherlands

Education in Human Rights Network,
Hugh Starkey, Secretary,
Westminster College,
Oxford, OX2 9AT,
United Kingdom

Teaching Tolerance,
Southern Poverty Law Centre,
400 Washington Avenue,
Mongomery, AL 36104,
United States

Quaker Peace Service,
Education Advisory Programme,
Friends' House,
Euston Road,
London NW1 2BJ,
United Kingdom

Extensive, Comprehensive, Computerized Bibliography On Peace Education,
Norman Richardson,
Inter-Church Centre,
48 Elmwood Avenue,
Belfast BT9 6AZ
United Kingdom

International Museum of Peace and Solidarity,
Attention: Anatoly Ionesov, Director
P.O. Box 76,
70300 Samarkand,
Uzbekistan

Education and Action for Peace Program,
Centro de Estudios Internacionales,
Apartado 1747,
Managua,
Nicaragua
E-mail: CEI@ nicarao.apc.org

Selected bibliography

Note: The majority of the titles listed here were mentioned and proposed by Member States in their replies to the circular letter of the Director-General of UNESCO concerning an elaborated version of the Integrated Action Plan for the Development of International Education, in particular materials proposed by Australia, Canada, Germany and New Zealand.

ANDERSON, A.; FRIDERES, J. *Ethnicity in Canada: Theoretical Perspectives.* Toronto, Butterworth, 1982.

BANKS, J. *Multiethnic Education: Theory and Practice.* New York, Allyn & Bacon, 1988.

BIRCH, B. *A Question of Race.* London, Macdonald, 1985.

BRAND, D.; KRISANTHA SRI BHAAGGIYADATTA. *Rivers Have Sources, Trees Have Roots.* Toronto, Cross Cultural Communication Centre, 1986.

BRANDT, G. L. *The Realization of Anti-racist Teaching.* London, Falmer Press, 1986.

CANADA. *Decade for Action to Combat Racism and Racial Discrimination, 1973–1983.* Ottawa, Secretary of State, Supply and Services Canada, 1978.

CIVIL SERVICE COMMISSION. *A Guide to Cross Cultural Issues: A Resource and Training Manual.* Vol. 2: *Prejudice, Discrimination and Values.* Winnipeg, Manitoba Civil Service Commission, Winnipeg Cross Cultural Consulting, 1987.

COUNCIL ON INTERRACIAL BOOKS FOR CHILDREN. *Childcare Shapes the Future: Anti-racist Strategies.* New York, Council on Interracial Books for Children, 1993.

——. *Counteracting Bias in Early Childhood Education,* Vol. 14, Nos. 7 and 8. New York, Council on Interracial Books for Children, 1983.

——. *Guidelines for Selecting Bias-free Textbooks and Storybooks.* New York, Council on Interracial Books for Children, 1987.

——. *Racism and Sexism in Children's Books.* Interracial Digest. Nos. 1 and 2. New York, Council on Interracial Books for Children, 1976, 1978.

CUMMINGS, M.A. (ed.). *Individual Differences: An Experience in Human Relations for Children: An Educator's Handbook for a Course of Studies about People.* Madison, Wis., Anti-Defamation League of B'nai B'Rith, 1974.

DIJK, T. A. *Communicating Racism: Ethnic Prejudice in Thought and Talk.* Newbury Park, Calif., Sage, 1986.

DOVIDIO, J. F.; GAERTNER, S. L. *Prejudice, Discrimination and Racism.* Orlando, Fla., Academic Press, 1986.

Éducation à la Paix. Textes fondamentaux pour l'éducation et l'action et la pochette de fiches de jeux. Paris, 1980.

Education for Human Dignity: Human Rights and Responsibility. Philadelphia, University of Pennsylvania Press, 1995.

Education for Justice. London, 1986.

GAY, K. *Bigotry.* Hillside, N.J., Enslow Publishers, 1989.

GUNDARA, J.; CRISPIN JONES (eds.). *Racism, Diversity and Education.* London/ Toronto, Hodder & Stoughton, 1986.

Handbook of Intercultural Training. Vols. 1, 2 and 3. New York/Oxford/ Toronto/Sydney/Paris/Frankfurt, 1987.

HESSARI, R.; HILL, D. *Practical Ideas for Multicultural Learning and Teaching in the Primary Classroom.* London, Routledge, 1989.

INSTITUTE FOR EDUCATIONAL RESEARCH. *Growth towards Peace and Environment Responsibility: Theory into Practice.* Institute for Educational Research, University of Yyväskylä (Finland), 1991.

KEHOE, J. *A Handbook for Enhancing the Multicultural Climate of the School.* Vancouver, B.C., Alternatives to Racism, The Western Educational Development Group, 1983.

LEE, E. *Letters to Marica: A Teacher's Guide to Anti-racist Education.* Toronto, Cross Cultural Communication Centre, 1985.

LYNCH, J. *Prejudice Reduction and the Schools.* London, Cassell, 1987.

MCLEAN, B.; YOUNG J. N. *Multicultural Anti-Racist Education: A Manual for Primary Schools.* London, Longmans, 1988.

MOODLEY, K. (ed.). *Race Relations and Multicultural Education.* University of British Columbia, Centre for the Study of Curriculum and Instruction, 1985.

MORTON, T.; MCBRIDE J. *Look Again: The Process of Prejudice and Discrimination.* Vancouver, B.C., CommCept Publishing, 1977.

Multicultural Education: Towards Good Practice. London, Boston & Henley, 1986.

NORTHWEST REGIONAL EDUCATIONAL LABORATORY. *Guide to Nonsexist Teaching Activities (K-12).* Phoenix, Arizona, The Oryx Press, 1983.

PREISWERK, R. *The Slant of the Pen: Racism in Children's Books.* Geneva, Office of Education, World Council of Churches, 1980.

Racism: Opposing Viewpoints. Revised edition. St. Paul, Minn., Greenlawn Press, 1986.

SCHERMERHORN, R. *Comparative Ethnic Relations: A Framework for Theory and Research.* Chicago, University of Chicago Press, 1978.

SCHNEIDEWIND, N. *Open Minds to Equality: A Sourcebook of Learning Activities to Promote Race, Sex, Class and Age Equality.* Englewood Cliffs, N.J./Toronto, Prentice-Hall, 1983.

SCHNIEDEWIND, N.; DAVIDSON, E. *Co-operative Learning, Co-operative Lives: A Sourcebook of Learning Activities for Building a Peaceful World.* Dubuque, Iowa, Wm C. Brown Co., 1987.

SHIMAN, D. A. *The Prejudice Book: Activities for the Classroom.* New York, Anti-Defamation League of B'nai B'rith, 1979.

SIMMS, R.; CONTRERAS, G. *Racism and Sexism: Responding to the Challenge.* New York, National Council for the Social Studies, 1980.

SIMON, R. I., et al. *Decoding Discrimination: A Student-based Approach to Anti-racist Education Using Film.* London, Ont. (Canada), University of Western Ontario/The Althouse Press, 1988.

SIMPSON, G.; YINGER, M. *Racial and Cultural Minorities.* New York, Harper & Row, 1965.

SLEETER, C. E.; GRANT, C. A. *Making Choices for Multicultural Education: Five Approaches to Race, Class and Gender.* Columbus, Ohio, Merrill, 1988.

STENHOUSE, L. V. G.; WILD, R. *Teaching about Race Relations: Problems and Effects.* London, Routledge & Kegan Paul, 1982.

UNESCO. *Peace and Conflict Issues after the Cold War.* Paris, UNESCO, 1992. (UNESCO Studies on Peace and Conflict.)

WILLIAMS, T.; MILLINOFF, H. *Canada's Schools: Report Card for the 1990s.* Ottawa, Canadian Education Association, 1990.

Some materials relevant to education for tolerance, peace, human rights and democracy published by UNESCO

Access to Human Rights Documentation. Paris, UNESCO, 1991.

Apartheid: A Teacher's Guide. Paris, UNESCO, 1981.

The Art of Living in Peace. By Pierre Weil. 1990.

Education, Culture, Human Rights, and International Understanding. By Francine Best, n.d.

Education Facing the Crisis of Values, Report Document. 1991.

Education for International Understanding, Co-operation, Peace and Human Rights. Bangkok, APEID, n.d.

An Experimental Project in Teaching Peace Studies by Distance Teaching Methods at STOU. 1990.

Human Rights, Questions and Answers. 3rd ed., rev. Paris, UNESCO, 1996.

International Education: Guidelines for Curriculum and Textbook Development in International Education. Paris, UNESCO, 1991 (doc. ED/ECS/HCI).

International Human Rights and International Education. Paris, UNESCO, 1976.

International Practical Guide on the Implementation of the 1974 UNESCO Recommendation. 1991.

Learning to Live in Security (Swedish Pilot Project on Peace, Disarmament, Security and Development). 1991.

No to Violence. Paris, UNESCO, 1997.

Teaching for International Understanding, Peace and Human Rights. Paris, UNESCO, 1984.

Materials produced by UNESCO's Associated Schools projects

Come Visit Our Country, Sweden. Other titles in English in the series deal with Bulgaria, India, Kenya, Morocco and Qatar.

Environmental Education for Our Common Future: A Handbook for Teachers in Europe. Oslo, Norwegian University Press, 1991.

Innovative Methods in the Associated Schools Project. Lise Tourtet (France), 1988.

International Understanding at School. Bulletin published twice a year, in English, French, Spanish and Arabic.

Key Words for Participating in the UNESCO Associated Schools Project. Practical Manual. Paris, UNESCO, 1997. In English and French; Spanish in preparation.

Looking at the ASP (Newsletter). Published in English, French, Spanish and Arabic.

The Role of Pre-school Education in International Understanding and Education for Peace. Paris, UNESCO, 1985 (reprinted 1989) (doc. ED-85/WS/11.)

Seeds for Peace, 1985.

Yes, We Can ... Together. Paris, UNESCO, 1987. In English, Spanish and Arabic.

Materials produced in co-operation with UNESCO's Associated Schools project

Continuing Challenges to Human Rights and Peace. Bulgaria, 1992.

International Understanding Through Foreign Language Teaching. Bonn, 1989.

Peace Primer. Pakistan, 1991.

World Concerns and the United Nations. New York, 1983.

Feature-length films produced for theatrical presentation now on video and available for sale or hire in most video shops

The listing is by the languages in which they were produced.

- Bengali (India)
  Salaam Bombay
  Two Daughters
- Chinese
  Five Girls on a Rope
  Raise the Red Lantern
  San Mao
  Le Petit Vagabond
- English (Australia)
  Where the Green Ants Dream
- English (Ireland)
  My Left Foot
- English (United Kingdom)
  Gandhi
  My Beautiful Laundrette
- English (United States)
  The Color Purple
  Columbus 1492
  Cry Freedom
  Dances with Wolves
  The Diary of Anne Frank
  Do the Right Thing
  Driving Miss Daisy
  A Dry White Season
  The Emerald Forest
  Far and Away
  Geronimo
  Holocaust
  Invisible Men
  Judgement at Nuremberg
  Julia

The Killing Fields
The Last of the Mohicans
A Long Walk Home
Malcolm X
Mandingo – Slavery in the USA
The Mission
Mississippi Burning
Mississippi Masala
Mosquito Coast
Native Son
Philadelphia
Raisin in the Sun
Roots – A History of Black People in the USA
Sarafina
Schindler's List
Sophie's Choice
- English (South Africa)
Place of Weeping
- French
Au Revoir les Enfants
Le Grand Bleu
La Haine
Indochina
Laisse Béton
Les 400 Coups
Sugar Cane Alley
- German
The Nasty Girl
- Greek
State of Siege
Z
- Italian
Galileo
Maicol
- Japanese
A River with No Bridge
- Ouagadougou
Karim and Sala
- Portuguese (Brazil)
Pixote
- Spanish (Argentina)
Official Story
- Spanish (Colombia)
Los Gambinos

- Spanish (Mexico)
  Los Olvidados
- Swedish
  Fannie and Alexander
- Turkish
  The Journey of Hope
  Ramparts of Clay

UNESCO films on the themes of tolerance, peace, war (produced between 1992 and 1994)

Felix Houphouet-Boigny Prize, 1993, Rabin, Perez, Arafat. Produced by UNESCO/OPI. French. 22 minutes.

From the Culture of War to the Culture of Peace. Produced for the fiftieth Anniversary of the United Nations. UNESCO/OPI. English, French, Spanish. 11 minutes.

International Forum on the Culture of Peace. UNESCO/OPI.

Teaching Emergency Package, Rwanda. TEP. English with French subtitles. 10 minutes.

United Nations Year for Tolerance. Produced by WTN. English, Spanish. 3 minutes, 24 seconds.

2. Declaration and Integrated Framework of Action on Education for Peace, Human Rights and Democracy

Declaration of the 44th session of the International Conference on Education

1. *We, the Ministers of Education* meeting at the 44th session of the International Conference on Education,

    Deeply concerned by the manifestations of violence, racism, xenophobia, aggressive nationalism and violations of human rights, by religious intolerance, by the upsurge of terrorism in all its forms and manifestations and by the growing gap separating wealthy countries from poor countries, phenomena which threaten the consolidation of peace and democracy both nationally and internationally and which are all obstacles to development,

    Mindful of our responsibility for the education of citizens committed to the promotion of peace, human rights and democracy in accordance with the letter and spirit of the Charter of the United Nations, the Constitution of UNESCO, the Universal Declaration of Human Rights and other relevant instruments such as the Convention on the Rights of the Child and the conventions on the rights of women, and in accordance with the Recommendation concerning Education for International Understanding, Co-operation and Peace and Education relating to Human Rights and Fundamental Freedoms,

    Convinced that education policies have to contribute to the development of understanding, solidarity and tolerance among individuals and among ethnic, social, cultural and religious groups and sovereign nations,

    Convinced that education should promote knowledge, values, attitudes and skills conducive to respect for human rights and to an active commitment to the defence of such rights and to the building of a culture of peace and democracy,

    Equally convinced:
    - of the great responsibility incumbent not only on parents, but on society as a whole, to work together with all those involved in the education system, and with non-governmental organizations, so as to achieve full implementation of the objectives of education for peace, human rights and democracy and to contribute in this way to sustainable development and to a culture of peace;

- of the need to seek synergies between the formal education system and the various sectors of non-formal education, which are helping to make a reality of education that is in conformity with the aims of the World Declaration on Education for All, adopted in Jomtien;
- of the decisive role that also falls to non-formal educational organizations in the process of forming the personalities of young people;

2.   *Strive resolutely:*

2.1 to base education on principles and methods that contribute to the development of the personality of pupils, students and adults who are respectful of their fellow human beings and determined to promote peace, human rights and democracy;

2.2 to take suitable steps to establish in educational institutions an atmosphere contributing to the success of education for international understanding, so that they become ideal places for the exercise of tolerance, respect for human rights, the practice of democracy and learning about the diversity and wealth of cultural identities;

2.3 to take action to eliminate all direct and indirect discrimination against girls and women in education systems and to take specific measures to ensure that they achieve their full potential;

2.4 to give special attention to improving curricula, the content of textbooks, and other educational materials including new technologies, with a view to educating caring and responsible citizens open to other cultures, able to appreciate the value of freedom, respectful of human dignity and differences, and able to prevent conflicts or resolve them by non-violent means;

2.5 to adopt measures to enhance the role and status of educators in formal and non-formal education and to give priority to pre-service and in-service training as well as the retraining of educational personnel, including planners and managers, oriented notably towards professional ethics, civic and moral education, cultural diversity, national codes and internationally recognized standards of human rights and fundamental freedoms;

2.6 to encourage the development of innovative strategies adapted to the new challenges of educating responsible citizens committed to peace, human rights, democracy and sustainable development, and to apply appropriate measures of evaluation and assessment of these strategies;

2.7 to prepare, as quickly as possible and taking into account the constitutional structures of each State, programmes of action for the implementation of this Declaration;

3.   *We are determined to increase our efforts to:*

3.1 give a major priority in education to children and young people, who are particularly vulnerable to incitements to intolerance, racism and xenophobia;

3.2 seek the co-operation of all possible partners who would be able to help teachers to link the education process more closely to real social life and transform it into the practice of tolerance and solidarity, respect for human rights, democracy and peace;

3.3 develop further, at the national and international levels, exchanges of educational experiences and research, direct contacts between students, teachers and researchers, school twinning arrangements and visits, with special attention to experimental schools such as UNESCO Associated Schools, to UNESCO Chairs, educational innovation networks and UNESCO Clubs and Associations;

3.4 implement the Declaration and Programme of Action of the World Conference on Human Rights (Vienna, June 1993) and the World Plan of Action on Education for Human Rights and Democracy adopted at the International Congress on Education for Human Rights and Democracy (Montreal, March 1993), and make the internationally recognized instruments in the field of human rights available to all educational establishments;

3.5 contribute, through specific activities, to the celebration of the United Nations Year for Tolerance (1995), and particularly to the inauguration, on the occasion of the fiftieth anniversary of the United Nations and UNESCO, of the celebration of the International Day for Tolerance.

Consequently, we, the Ministers of Education meeting at the 44th session of the International Conference on Education, *adopt* this Declaration and *invite* the Director-General to present to the General Conference a Framework of Action that allows Member States and UNESCO to integrate, within a coherent policy, education for peace, human rights and democracy in the perspective of sustainable development.

Integrated Framework of Action on Education for Peace, Human Rights and Democracy, approved by the General Conference of UNESCO at its twenty-eighth session, Paris, November 1995

I. Introduction

1.   This Integrated Framework of Action on Education for Peace, Human Rights and Democracy is intended to give effect to the Declaration adopted at the 44th session of the International Conference on Education. It suggests basic guidelines which could be translated into strategies, policies and plans of action at the institutional and national levels according to the conditions of different communities.

2.   In a period of transition and accelerated change marked by the expression of intolerance, manifestations of racial and ethnic hatred, the upsurge of terrorism in all its forms and manifestations, discrimination, war and violence towards those regarded as 'other' and the growing disparities between rich and poor, at international and national levels alike, action strategies must aim both at ensuring fundamental freedoms, peace, human rights, and democracy and at promoting sustainable and equitable economic and social development, all of which have an

essential part to play in building a culture of peace. This calls for a transformation of the traditional styles of educational action.

3. The international community has recently expressed its firm resolve to provide itself with instruments adapted to the current challenges in the world in order to act in a concerted and effective way. The Vienna Declaration and Programme of Action for Human Rights adopted by the World Conference on Human Rights (Vienna, June 1993), the World Plan of Action on Education for Human Rights and Democracy adopted by the International Congress on Education for Human Rights and Democracy (Montreal, March 1993), and the Associated Schools Project Strategy and Plan of Action 1994-2000 are, in this respect, attempts to respond to the challenge of promoting peace, human rights, democracy and development.

4. Taking inspiration from the Recommendation on Education for International Understanding, Co-operation and Peace and Education relating to Human Rights and Fundamental Freedoms, this Framework of Action seeks to suggest to Member States and international governmental and non-governmental organizations an up-to-date and integrated view of problems and strategies concerning education for peace, human rights and democracy. It was drawn up at the request of the General Conference at its twenty-seventh session, taking into account existing action plans, and its purpose is to enhance their practical relevance and effectiveness. The idea then is to draw on accumulated experience in order to chart new directions for the education of citizens in every country. The Framework of Action accordingly identifies principles and objectives of action and formulates proposals for the consideration of policy-makers within each State and for co-operation between countries on the basis of the commitments contained in the Declaration, to which it is closely linked. It also attempts to bring together into a coherent whole the various measures aimed at defining study topics, realigning education at all levels, rethinking methods and reviewing teaching materials in use, stimulating research, developing teacher training and helping to make the education system more open to society by means of active partnership.

5. All human rights are universal, indivisible, interdependent and interrelated. The strategies of action for their implementation must take specific historic, religious and cultural considerations into account.

II. Aims of education for peace, human rights and democracy

6. The ultimate goal of education for peace, human rights and democracy is the development in every individual of a sense of universal values and types of behaviour on which a culture of peace is predicated. It is possible to identify even in different socio-cultural contexts values that are likely to be universally recognized.

7. Education must develop the ability to value freedom and the skills to meet its challenges. This means preparing citizens to cope with difficult and uncertain situations and fitting them for personal autonomy and responsibility. Awareness of personal responsibility must be linked to recognition of the value of civic

commitment, of joining together with others to solve problems and to work for a just, peaceful and democratic community.

8. Education must develop the ability to recognize and accept the values which exist in the diversity of individuals, genders, peoples and cultures and develop the ability to communicate, share and co-operate with others. The citizens of a pluralist society and multicultural world should be able to accept that their interpretation of situations and problems is rooted in their personal lives, in the history of their society and in their cultural traditions; that, consequently, no individual or group holds the only answer to problems; and that for each problem there may be more than one solution. Therefore, people should understand and respect each other and negotiate on an equal footing, with a view to seeking common ground. Thus education must reinforce personal identity and should encourage the convergence of ideas and solutions which strengthen peace, friendship and solidarity between individuals and people.

9. Education must develop the ability of non-violent conflict-resolution. It should therefore promote also the development of inner peace in the minds of students so that they can establish more firmly the qualities of tolerance, compassion, sharing and caring.

10. Education must cultivate in citizens the ability to make informed choices, basing their judgements and actions not only on the analysis of present situations but also on the vision of a preferred future.

11. Education must teach citizens to respect the cultural heritage, protect the environment, and adopt methods of production and patterns of consumption which lead to sustainable development. Harmony between individual and collective values and between immediate basic needs and long-term interests is also necessary.

12. Education should cultivate feelings of solidarity and equity at the national and international levels in the perspective of a balanced and long-term development.

III. Strategies

13. In order to achieve these aims, the strategies and forms of action of education systems will clearly need to be modified, as necessary, in respect both of teaching and of administration. Furthermore, providing basic education for all and promoting the rights of women as an integral and indivisible part of universal human rights are fundamental in education for peace, human rights and democracy.

14. Strategies relating to education for peace, human rights and democracy must:
   (a) be comprehensive and holistic, which means addressing a very broad range of factors some of which are described in more detail below;
   (b) be applicable to all types, levels and forms of education;
   (c) involve all educational partners and various agents of socialization, including NGOs and community organizations;
   (d) be implemented locally, nationally, regionally and worldwide;
   (e) entail modes of management and administration, co-ordination and assessment that give greater autonomy to educational establishments so that they can work out specific forms of action and linkage with the local community, encourage

the development of innovations and foster active and democratic participation by all those concerned in the life of the establishment;

(f) be suited to the age and psychology of the target group and take account of the evolution of the learning capacity of each individual;

(g) be applied on a continuous and consistent basis. Results and obstacles have to be assessed, in order to ensure that strategies can be continuously adapted to changing circumstances;

(h) include proper resources for the above aims, for education as a whole and especially for marginalized and disadvantaged groups.

15. The degree of change required, priorities for action and the sequence of actions should be determined at all decision-making levels taking into account different historical backgrounds, cultural traditions and development levels of regions and countries, and even within countries.

IV. Policies and lines of action

16. The incorporation into curricula at all levels of education, formal and non-formal, of lessons on peace, human rights and democracy is of crucial importance.

Content of education

17. To strengthen the formation of values and abilities such as solidarity, creativity, civic responsibility, the ability to resolve conflicts by non-violent means, and critical acumen, it is necessary to introduce into curricula, at all levels, true education for citizenship which includes an international dimension. Teaching should particularly concern the conditions for the construction of peace; the various forms of conflict, their causes and effects; the ethical, religious and philosophical bases of human rights, their historical sources, the way they have developed and how they have been translated into national and international standards, such as in the Universal Declaration of Human Rights, the Convention on the Elimination of All Forms of Discrimination against Women and the Convention on the Rights of the Child; the bases of democracy and its various institutional models; the problem of racism and the history of the fight against sexism and all the other forms of discrimination and exclusion. Particular attention should be devoted to culture, the problem of development and the history of every people, as well as to the role of the United Nations and international institutions. There must be education for peace, human rights and democracy. It cannot, however, be restricted to specialized subjects and knowledge. The whole of education must transmit this message and the atmosphere of the institution must be in harmony with the application of democratic standards. Likewise, curriculum reform should emphasize knowledge, understanding and respect for the culture of others at the national and global levels and should link the global interdependence of problems to local action. In view of religious and cultural differences, every country may decide which approach to ethical education best suits its cultural context.

Teaching materials and resources

18.   All people engaged in educational action must have adequate teaching materials and resources at their disposal. In this connection, it is necessary to make the necessary revisions to textbooks to remove negative stereotypes and distorted views of 'the other'. International co-operation in producing textbooks could be encouraged. Whenever new teaching materials, textbooks and the like are to be produced, they should be designed with due consideration of new situations. The textbooks should offer different perspectives on a given subject and make transparent the national or cultural background against which they are written. Their content should be based on scientific findings. It would be desirable for the documents of UNESCO and other United Nations institutions to be widely distributed and used in educational establishments, especially in countries where the production of teaching materials is proving slow owing to economic difficulties. Distance education technologies and all modern communication tools must be placed at the service of education for peace, human rights and democracy.

Programmes for reading, expression and the promotion of foreign languages

19.   It is essential for the development of education for peace, human rights and democracy that reading and verbal and written expression programmes should be considerably strengthened. A comprehensive grasp of reading, writing and the spoken word enables citizens to gain access to information, to understand clearly the situation in which they are living, to express their needs, and to take part in activities in the social environment. In the same way, learning foreign languages offers a means of gaining a deeper understanding of other cultures, which can serve as a basis for building better understanding between communities and between nations. UNESCO's LINGUAPAX project could serve as an example in that respect.

Educational establishments

20.   Proposals for educational change find their natural place in schools and classrooms. Teaching and learning methods, forms of action and institutional policy lines have to make peace, human rights and democracy both a matter of daily practice and something that is learned. With regard to methods, the use of active methods, group work, the discussion of moral issues and personalized teaching should be encouraged. As for institutional policy lines, efficient forms of management and participation must promote the implementation of democratic school management, involving teachers, pupils, parents and the local community as a whole.

21.   Direct contacts and regular exchanges should be promoted between pupils, students, teachers and other educators in different countries or cultural environments, and visits should be organized to establishments where successful experiments and innovations have been carried out, particularly between neighbouring countries. Joint projects should be implemented between establishments and institutions from different countries, with a view to solving common problems. International networks of pupils, students and researchers working towards the same objectives should also be set up. Such networks should,

as a matter of priority, ensure that schools in particularly difficult situations due to extreme poverty or insecurity should take part in them. With this in mind, it is essential to strengthen and develop the UNESCO Associated Schools System. All these activities, within the limits of available resources, should be introduced as an integral component of teaching programmes.

22.   The reduction of failure must be a priority. Therefore, education should be adapted to the individual student's potential. The development of self-esteem, as well as strengthening the will to succeed in learning, are also basic necessities for achieving a higher degree of social integration. Greater autonomy for schools implies greater responsibility on the part of teachers and the community for the results of education. However, the different development levels of education systems should determine the degree of autonomy in order to avoid a possible weakening of educational content.

Teacher training

23.   The training of personnel at all levels of the education system - teachers, planners, managers, teacher educators - has to include education for peace, human rights and democracy. This pre-service and in-service training and retraining should introduce and apply *in situ* methodologies, observing experiments and evaluating their results. In order to perform their tasks successfully, schools, institutions of teacher education and those in charge of non-formal education programmes should seek the assistance of people with experience in the fields of peace, human rights and democracy (politicians, jurists, sociologists and psychologists) and of the NGOs specialized in human rights. Similarly, pedagogy and the actual practice of exchanges should form part of the training courses of all educators.

24.   Teacher education activities must fit into an overall policy to upgrade the teaching profession. International experts, professional bodies and teachers' unions should be associated with the preparation and implementation of action strategies because they have an important role to play in promoting a culture of peace among teachers themselves.

Action on behalf of vulnerable groups

25.   Specific strategies for the education of vulnerable groups and those recently exposed to conflict or in a situation of open conflict are required as a matter of urgency, giving particular attention to children at risk and to girls and women subjected to sexual abuse and other forms of violence. Possible practical measures could include, for example, the organization outside the conflict zone of specialized forums and workshops for educators, family members and mass media professionals belonging to the conflicting groups and an intensive training activity for educators in post-conflict situations. Such measures should be undertaken in co-operation with governments whenever possible.

26.   The organization of education programmes for abandoned children, street children, refugee and displaced children and economically and sexually exploited children are a matter of urgency.

27.   It is equally urgent to organize special youth programmes laying emphasis on participation by children and young people in solidarity actions and environmental protection.

28.   In addition, efforts should be made to address the special needs of people with learning difficulties by providing them with relevant education in a non-exclusionary and integrated educational setting.

29.   Furthermore, in order to create understanding between different groups in society, there must be respect for the educational rights of persons belonging to national or ethnic, religious and linguistic minorities, as well as indigenous people, and this must also have implications in the curricula and methods and in the way education is organized.

Research and development

30.   New problems require new solutions. It is essential to work out strategies for making better use of research findings, to develop new teaching methods and approaches and to improve co-ordination in choosing research themes between research institutes in the social sciences and education in order to address in a more relevant and effective way the complex nature of education for peace, human rights and democracy. The effectiveness of educational management should be enhanced by research on decision-making by all those involved in the educational process (government, teachers, parents, etc.). Research should also be focused on finding new ways of changing public attitudes towards human rights, in particular towards women, and environmental issues. The impact of educational programmes may be better assessed by developing a system of indicators of results, setting up data banks on innovative experiments, and strengthening systems for disseminating and sharing information and research findings, nationally and internationally.

Higher education

31.   Higher education institutions can contribute in many ways to education for peace, human rights and democracy. In this connection, the introduction into the curricula of knowledge, values and skills relating to peace, human rights, justice, the practice of democracy, professional ethics, civic commitment and social responsibility should be envisaged. Educational institutions at this level should also ensure that students appreciate the interdependence of States in an increasingly global society.

Co-ordination between the education sector and other agents of socialization

32.   The education of citizens cannot be the exclusive responsibility of the education sector. If it is to be able to do its job effectively in this field, the education sector should closely co-operate, in particular, with the family, the media, including traditional channels of communication, the world of work and NGOs.

33.   Concerning co-ordination between school and family, measures should be taken to encourage the participation of parents in school activities. Furthermore, education programmes for adults and the community in general in order to strengthen the school's work are essential.

34.   The influence of the media in the socialization of children and young people is increasingly being acknowledged. It is, therefore, essential to train teachers and prepare students for the critical analysis and use of the media, and to develop their competence to profit from the media by a selective choice of programmes. On the other hand, the media should be urged to promote the values of peace, respect for human rights, democracy and tolerance, in particular by avoiding programmes and other products that incite hatred, violence, cruelty and disrespect for human dignity.

Non-formal education of young people and adults

35.   Young people who spend a lot of time outside school and who often do not have access to the formal education system, or to vocational training or a job, as well as young people doing their military service, are a very important target group of education programmes for peace, human rights and democracy. While seeking improved access to formal education and vocational training, it is therefore essential for them to be able to receive non-formal education adapted to their needs, which would prepare them to assume their role as citizens in a responsible and effective way. In addition, education for peace, human rights and respect for the law has to be provided for young people in prisons, reformatories or treatment centres.

36.   Adult education programmes - in which NGOs have an important role to play - should make everyone aware of the link between local living conditions and world problems. Basic education programmes should attach particular importance to subject-matter relating to peace, human rights and democracy. All culturally suitable media such as folklore, popular theatre, community discussion groups and radio should be used in mass education.

Regional and international co-operation

37.   The promotion of peace and democracy will require regional co-operation, international solidarity and the strengthening of co-operation between international and governmental bodies, non-governmental organizations, the scientific community, business circles, industry and the media. This solidarity and co-operation must help the developing countries to meet their needs for promoting education for peace, human rights and democracy.

38.   UNESCO should place its institutional capability, and in particular its regional and international innovation networks, in the service of the efforts to give effect to this Framework of Action. The Associated Schools Project, the UNESCO Clubs and Associations, the UNESCO Chairs, the major education projects for Africa, Asia and the Pacific, Latin America and the Caribbean, the Arab States and Europe, the follow-up bodies of the Jomtien World Conference, and in particular the regional and international conferences of ministers of education should make specific contributions. In these efforts, especially at national level, the active participation of National Commissions for UNESCO should be a strategic asset in enhancing the effectiveness of the actions proposed.

39.   UNESCO should introduce questions relating to the application of this Framework of Action at meetings to be held at the highest level regionally and internationally, develop programmes for the training of educational personnel, strengthen or develop networks of institutions, and carry out comparative research on teaching programmes, methods and materials. In accordance with the commitments set forth in the Declaration on Education for Peace, Human Rights and Democracy, the programmes should be evaluated on a regular basis.

40.   In this context, UNESCO, in line with such United Nations actions as 'Agenda for Peace', 'Agenda for Development', 'Agenda 21', 'Social Summit' and 'the Fourth World Conference on Women', should launch initiatives to implement this operation with other institutions in the United Nations system and other regional and international organizations, so as to establish a global plan of activities and set priorities for joint, co-ordinated action. This could include a UNESCO-managed fund for international co-operation in education for peace, human rights and democracy.

41.   National and international non-governmental organizations should be encouraged to participate actively in the implementation of this Framework of Action.

3. Declaration of Principles on Tolerance[1]

The Member States of the United Nations Educational, Scientific and Cultural Organization,
meeting in Paris at the twenty-eighth session of the General Conference, from
25 October to 16 November 1995,

Preamble

Bearing in mind that the United Nations Charter states: 'We, the peoples of the United
Nations determined to save succeeding generations from the scourge of war, . . .
to reaffirm faith in fundamental human rights, in the dignity and worth of the
human person, . . . and for these ends to practise tolerance and live together in
peace with one another as good neighbours',

Recalling that the Preamble to the Constitution of UNESCO, adopted on 16 November
1945, states that 'peace, if it is not to fail, must be founded on the intellectual and
moral solidarity of mankind',

Recalling also that the Universal Declaration of Human Rights affirms that 'Everyone has
the right to freedom of thought, conscience and religion' (Article 18), 'of opinion
and expression' (Article 19), and that education 'should promote understanding,
tolerance and friendship among all nations, racial or religious groups' (Article 26),

Noting relevant international instruments including:
- the International Covenant on Civil and Political Rights,
- the International Covenant on Economic, Social and Cultural Rights,
- the Convention on the Elimination of All Forms of Racial Discrimination,
- the Convention on the Prevention and Punishment of the Crime of Genocide,
- the Convention on the Rights of the Child,
- the 1951 Convention relating to the Status of Refugees and its 1967 Protocol
  and regional instruments,
- the Convention on the Elimination of All Forms of Discrimination against
  Women,

---

1. Proclaimed and signed on 16 November 1995.

- the Convention against Torture and other Cruel, Inhuman or Degrading Treatment or Punishment,
- the Declaration on the Elimination of All Forms of Intolerance Based on Religion or Belief,
- the Declaration on the Rights of Persons Belonging to National or Ethnic, Religious and Linguistic Minorities,
- the Declaration on Measures to Eliminate International Terrorism,
- the Vienna Declaration and Programme of Action of the World Conference on Human Rights,
- the Copenhagen Declaration and Programme of Action adopted by the World Summit for Social Development,
- the UNESCO Declaration on Race and Racial Prejudice,
- the UNESCO Convention and Recommendation against Discrimination in Education,

Bearing in mind the objectives of the Third Decade to Combat Racism and Racial Discrimination, the World Decade for Human Rights Education, and the International Decade of the World's Indigenous People,

Taking into consideration the recommendations of regional conferences organized in the framework of the United Nations Year for Tolerance in accordance with UNESCO General Conference 27 C/Resolution 5.14, as well as the conclusions and recommendations of other conferences and meetings organized by Member States within the programme of the United Nations Year for Tolerance,

Alarmed by the current rise in acts of intolerance, violence, terrorism, xenophobia, aggressive nationalism, racism, anti-Semitism, exclusion, marginalization and discrimination directed against national, ethnic, religious and linguistic minorities, refugees, migrant workers, immigrants and vulnerable groups within societies, as well as acts of violence and intimidation committed against individuals exercising their freedom of opinion and expression - all of which threaten the consolidation of peace and democracy, both nationally and internationally, and are obstacles to development,

Emphasizing the responsibilities of Member States to develop and encourage respect for human rights and fundamental freedoms for all, without distinction as to race, gender, language, national origin, religion or disability, and to combat intolerance,

Adopt and solemnly proclaim this Declaration of Principles on Tolerance

Resolving to take all positive measures necessary to promote tolerance in our societies, because tolerance is not only a cherished principle, but also a necessity for peace and for the economic and social advancement of all peoples,

We declare the following:

Article 1. Meaning of tolerance

1.1   Tolerance is respect, acceptance and appreciation of the rich diversity of our world's cultures, our forms of expression and ways of being human. It is fostered by knowledge, openness, communication, and freedom of thought, conscience and belief. Tolerance is harmony in difference. It is not only a moral duty, it is also a political and legal requirement. Tolerance, the virtue that makes peace possible, contributes to the replacement of the culture of war by a culture of peace.

1.2   Tolerance is not concession, condescension or indulgence. Tolerance is, above all, an active attitude prompted by recognition of the universal human rights and fundamental freedoms of others. In no circumstance can it be used to justify infringements of these fundamental values. Tolerance is to be exercised by individuals, groups and States.

1.3   Tolerance is the responsibility that upholds human rights, pluralism (including cultural pluralism), democracy and the rule of law. It involves the rejection of dogmatism and absolutism and affirms the standards set out in international human rights instruments.

1.4   Consistent with respect for human rights, the practice of tolerance does not mean toleration of social injustice or the abandonment or weakening of one's convictions. It means that one is free to adhere to one's own convictions and accepts that others adhere to theirs. It means accepting the fact that human beings, naturally diverse in their appearance, situation, speech, behaviour and values, have the right to live in peace and to be as they are. It also means that one's views are not to be imposed on others.

Article 2. State level

2.1   Tolerance at the State level requires just and impartial legislation, law enforcement and judicial and administrative process. It also requires that economic and social opportunities be made available to each person without any discrimination. Exclusion and marginalization can lead to frustration, hostility and fanaticism.

2.2   In order to achieve a more tolerant society, States should ratify existing international human rights conventions, and draft new legislation where necessary to ensure equality of treatment and of opportunity for all groups and individuals in society.

2.3   It is essential for international harmony that individuals, communities and nations accept and respect the multicultural character of the human family. Without tolerance there can be no peace, and without peace there can be no development or democracy.

2.4   Intolerance may take the form of marginalization of vulnerable groups and their exclusion from social and political participation, as well as violence and discrimination against them. As confirmed in the Declaration on Race and Racial Prejudice, 'All individuals and groups have the right to be different' (Article 1.2).

Article 3. Social dimensions

3.1   In the modern world, tolerance is more essential than ever before. It is an age marked by the globalization of the economy and by rapidly increasing mobility, communication, integration and interdependence, large-scale migrations and displacement of populations, urbanization and changing social patterns. Since every part of the world is characterized by diversity, escalating intolerance and strife potentially menaces every region. It is not confined to any country, but is a global threat.

3.2 Tolerance is necessary between individuals and at the family and community levels. Tolerance promotion and the shaping of attitudes of openness, mutual listening and solidarity should take place in schools and universities and through non-formal education, at home and in the workplace. The communication media are in a position to play a constructive role in facilitating free and open dialogue and discussion, disseminating the values of tolerance, and highlighting the dangers of indifference towards the rise in intolerant groups and ideologies.

3.3 As affirmed by the UNESCO Declaration on Race and Racial Prejudice, measures must be taken to ensure equality in dignity and rights for individuals and groups wherever necessary. In this respect, particular attention should be paid to vulnerable groups which are socially or economically disadvantaged so as to afford them the protection of the laws and social measures in force, in particular with regard to housing, employment and health, to respect the authenticity of their culture and values, and to facilitate their social and occupational advancement and integration, especially through education.

3.4 Appropriate scientific studies and networking should be undertaken to co-ordinate the international community's response to this global challenge, including analysis by the social sciences of root causes and effective countermeasures, as well as research and monitoring in support of policy-making and standard-setting action by Member States.

Article 4. Education

4.1 Education is the most effective means of preventing intolerance. The first step in tolerance education is to teach people what their shared rights and freedoms are, so that they may be respected, and to promote the will to protect those of others.

4.2 Education for tolerance should be considered an urgent imperative; that is why it is necessary to promote systematic and rational tolerance teaching methods that will address the cultural, social, economic, political and religious sources of intolerance – major roots of violence and exclusion. Education policies and programmes should contribute to development of understanding, solidarity and tolerance among individuals as well as among ethnic, social, cultural, religious and linguistic groups and nations.

4.3 Education for tolerance should aim at countering influences that lead to fear and exclusion of others, and should help young people to develop capacities for independent judgement, critical thinking and ethical reasoning.

4.4 We pledge to support and implement programmes of social science research and education for tolerance, human rights and non-violence. This means devoting special attention to improving teacher training, curricula, the content of textbooks and lessons, and other educational materials including new educational technologies, with a view to educating caring and responsible citizens open to other cultures, able to appreciate the value of freedom, respectful of human dignity and differences, and able to prevent conflicts or resolve them by non-violent means.

Article 5. Commitment to action

    We commit ourselves to promoting tolerance and non-violence through programmes and institutions in the fields of education, science, culture and communication.

Article 6. International Day for Tolerance

    In order to generate public awareness, emphasize the dangers of intolerance and react with renewed commitment and action in support of tolerance promotion and education, we solemnly proclaim 16 November the annual International Day for Tolerance.